Springfield Cambridge Bishopbriggs

The story of a church

Bill Findlay

© Bill Findlay, 2005

Published by
William Findlay
36 Firpark Road,
Bishopbriggs,
Glasgow, G64 1SP
Telephone: 0141 772 7253

Printed by
Cordfall Ltd, Glasgow, 0141 572 0878

ISBN 0 9551574 0 4

I would like to dedicate this book to all members of
Springfield Cambridge Church, past, present and future.
Also to the memory of my parents
and to my long time friend, the late Betty McNicol.

Acknowledgements

I would like to thank the members of Springfield Cambridge Church who assisted me by providing information relating to various organisations etc. Special thanks to Jim McGeachie, Willie Minto and Malcolm Galston.

I would also like to thank Don Martin and the staff of William Patrick Library, East Dunbartonshire.

Illustrations of old and new churches are from originals by James Woods.

Foreword

The main purpose of my writing this book is to record the history of a church. I have also attempted to outline the impact of local, national and international events on church life.

Contents

Chapter 1	**The man from Unst**	7
Chapter 2	**What's in a name?**	11
Chapter 3	**A new age dawns**	13
Chapter 4	**People of note**	15
Chapter 5	**Men of parts**	18
Chapter 6	**Difficult times**	20
Chapter 7	**Growth and reunion**	23
Chapter 8	**Gathering clouds**	26
Chapter 9	**War years**	29
Chapter 10	**Problems and opportunities**	32
Chapter 11	**Ups and downs**	35
Chapter 12	**Downs and ups**	37
Chapter 13	**Onwards and upwards**	38
Chapter 14	**Triumph and tragedy**	42
Chapter 15	**Moving forward**	44
Chapter 16	**Basis of union**	47
Chapter 17	**Union and progress**	49
Chapter 18	**The wind of change**	52
Chapter 19	**The new minister**	55
Chapter 20	**Looking back, looking forward**	58
Chapter 21	**Towards the millennium**	61
Chapter 22	**2000 and beyond**	63
	Sources	65
	Index	66

Chapter 1
The man from Unst

Rudyard Kipling kept six honest serving men whose names were Where and What and Why and When and How and Who. They have been employed by many writers before and since, and to the historian they are indispensable. The story goes that a man was driving from Glasgow to Edinburgh, got hopelessly lost, and found himself in Bishopbriggs. He asked a local for directions, to which the answer was-

"Edinburgh? Well if I were you I wouldn't start from here."

When writing a history it is always difficult to know just where to begin. 1865 (more later) would be a possible date. This would certainly employ one of our serving men, WHEN, but let us dig more deeply.

The hymn writer, Samuel John Stone, tells us that "The Church's one foundation is Jesus Christ her Lord". This reminds us that the church is more than bricks and mortar. Another hymn writer, Carol Rose Ikeler, says that "The Church is wherever God's people are praising". Let us, therefore, begin with people.

The Gospel was brought to Scotland by a number of Christians. Some have been forgotten, others such as Ninian, Kessog and Columba are remembered to this day. Another well remembered saint was Mungo (or Kentigern) who founded the church of Glasgow. Centuries later, that church established a daughter church at Cadder. Both adhered to the Roman Catholic tradition until the Reformation.

In 1560 the Scottish Parliament adopted Protestantism as its national religion. Cadder church accepted the new tradition. It remained loyal to the Church of Scotland following the First Secession in 1733. In 1747 the Secession church divided into Burgher and Anti-Burgher. A further break away from the national church took place in 1761 when the Relief Church was formed. Cadder still remained loyal to the Church of Scotland.

In 1843 the Disruption took place when a considerable number of ministers and elders walked out of the General Assembly of the Church of Scotland to form a church which would be free of state control, i.e. the Free Church of Scotland. This movement spread throughout the country, and congregations were divided. Cadder was no exception.

Those who left attempted to establish a Free Church in Bishopbriggs. For a time they met in a barn at Bearyards farm (where the water tower now stands). Heating and lighting presented problems, as did the presence of vermin. Local landlords were hostile towards the Free Church, so its members could not find a site to build on. Eventually the church in the barn ceased to meet.

In the 1859, Bridgegate Free Church, Glasgow, set up a mission in what had been licensed premises in Auchinairn. This mission attracted, among others, people who had been members of Bishopbriggs Free Church. The mission continued to meet into the early 1860s.

A rather remarkable young man was appointed missionary in 1862. His name was James Fordyce. James, son of a sea captain and a devout Christian mother, left his home on the Shetland Island of Unst when he was about 16 or 17 to become a pupil of Glasgow High School. He then studied divinity at Glasgow University.

The Auchinairn mission prospered, and members were keen for it to become a church. A site was procured in Springfield Road, Bishopbriggs through the good offices of one of its members, James Cleland. Building began in 1863.

On 4 January 1865, the congregation petitioned Glasgow Presbytery requesting full church status. Presbytery agreed at their meeting on 1 February. This was sanctioned by the General Assembly on 30 May 1865, at which point Cadder Free Church came into being.

Old Church, from an original by J. Woods.

It is hardly surprising that when the Presbytery met in the new Cadder Free Church on 25 August 1865, it was to moderate a call for Rev. James Fordyce to become minister of the said church. He was ordained on 28 September 1865. Rev. Fordyce married a local lady, Miss Galloway, formerly of Huntershill.

By all accounts, Rev. Fordyce carried out his pastoral and ministerial duties in a dedicated and skilful manner. He became a member of Cadder School Board and it was he who performed the opening ceremony at the new Auchinairn School in 1876. That school is now the Community Hall.

Perhaps it was his Shetland upbringing that gave Rev. Fordyce a lifelong interest in nature, botany and astronomy. On his semi-jubilee in 1890, he was presented with an astronomical telescope. His main interest, however, was the church, to which he was devoted. It was he, together with others, who arranged the purchase of the Manse in Springfield Road. The title deeds for the ground were signed on 28 October 1868, the land being purchased from a Mrs Cleland for £750. A condition of the sale was that building/buildings there on be used as a Manse in all time coming.

The names of the trustees make interesting reading as they are indicative of the occupations of church leaders at that time. In addition to Rev. Fordyce's there was William Hamilton (Music publisher) and James Spittal (Farmer at Wester Lumloch), Elders; James Cleland (Factor), William Neilson (Farmer at Myrie-Mailing) and William Johnston (Blacksmith at Old Auchinairn), Deacons.

Rev. Fordyce continued to serve the church well in the years that followed. It was perhaps his devotion to duty that shortened his life. He caught a chill while conducting an outdoor service, took ill and died on 23 October 1891. He was minister for 26 years and 25 days.

On the day of Rev. James Fordyce's funeral, all shops in Auchinairn and Bishopbriggs closed as a mark of respect. Members of the public followed the cortege on foot to Colston Toll. Thereafter interment took place at Glasgow Necropolis.

The following poem goes a long way to summing up the life of a rather wonderful pastor and family man.

> Another pastor of renown,
> In mid-time of his day cut down
> Rich promise of his church he gave,
> Of yeoman service, bright and brave.
>
> From farthest isles of Scotia's north,
> With gospel zeal he sallied forth.
> Out from the city's swelling throng
> He plants the standard, firm and strong.
>
> In yonder rising village nigh,
> For six and twenty years gone by,

Aloft did lift that all might see,
The flag of truth, so full and free.

Gentle and meek, went in and out,
A smiling word for all about.
To poor afflicted folk so kind,
His footsteps gleamed with love behind.

In every path, home and abroad,
The minister and the man of God.
To win to Jesus souls he sought,
His grandest trophy, those he bought.

Dear to his flock he gathered there,
For him they wrestled oft in prayer.
That from his couch of sickness sore,
The Lord would him to them restore.

Alas the sands of life were run,
The servant's work on earth was done.
Lament the loved ones round his bed,
Their truest, fondest friend is dead.

Well done, good pastor of the sheep,
Thy master trusted thee to keep.
May thee and thine at great last day,
The Christ lead forth in bright array.

Footnote 1.
Bishopbriggs was not the only place where land owners refused to allow the Free Church land to build on. The people of Strontian had a floating church built. It was moored on Loch Sunart, had a seating capacity of 750, and served the congregation for more than 40 years.

Footnote 2.
Certain Burgesses were required to take an oath acknowledging 'the true religion presently professed within this realm'. Some saw this as implying an acknowledgment of the established Church, while others did not. Hence the dispute between Burghers and Anti-Burghers.

Chapter 2
What's in a name?

Actually names are quite important. Para Handy once said, "I forget your face but I remember your name". While you are working that one out let us consider some of our local place names. It is generally accepted that 'Auchinairn' means 'Fields of Iron'. On the other hand, the meaning of 'Bishopbriggs' is occasionally disputed. Some say that the name is derived from Bishop's Rigs, or 'fields of the Bishop'. Most people agree, however, that it comes from 'Bishop's Bridge'. The bridge referred to was the bridge across the Callie burn, now known as Bishopbriggs burn. Presumably the original bridge was built by the Bishop of Glasgow. Actually, a very old bridge is still in existence. It was preserved, out of sight, when the road was reconstructed a number of years ago.

At the end of the nineteenth century, in addition to Auchinairn, Bishopbriggs, Cadder and Lochfaulds, there were two other villages in the district: Mavis Valley, beyond the canal, and Jellyhill, at the foot of Balmuildy Road. They were mining villages while Bishopbriggs itself was occupied by a mixture of miners, former railway construction workers, quarry men, farm hands etc. It was a rough place then, and a visiting minister to Springfield Church during the 1950s informed the congregation that his parents left Bishopbriggs as they felt safer in nearby Springburn. From a social point of view, Bishopbriggs was a bit of a back water, or so it would seem.

Towards the end of the nineteenth century, however, things began to change. New houses were being built and "Sleeping Hollow" as the community was then known, was beginning to awake. The population rose from 934 in 1891 to 4743 in 1901. While this was going on, a successful young business man by the name of William Lindsay considered entering the ministry. After due consultation with Rev. James Barr, he under went the necessary training and on 31 March 1892, he was elected minister of Cadder Free church, then popularly known as Bishopbriggs Free Church.

Rev. Lindsay was ordained on 19 June. He brought about a number of changes such as introducing hymns to worship. This met with little resistance. The same cannot be said for his second innovation. In those days the congregation would sit to sing psalms and stand while the minister led them in prayer. Rev. Lindsay decided to reverse this procedure. One older member dissented and continued to stand during prayers. He was supported by a number of others whose names have been lost to posterity, except for the last two ladies to hold to the older tradition. They were Mrs Love and Mrs Stark, both of Auchinairn. One of them when challenged said, "I'll sit at the prayer when the minister sits". Rev. Lindsay took this in good part. It is interesting to note that the oldest surviving record pertaining to the church dates back to

Rev. Lindsay's term of office. It is the Baptismal Record (1894-1921), and is held in the Archives And Special Collections Section of the Mitchell Library. (Catalogued CH3/1164/12)

The community continued to grow. A new school was opened at Bishopbriggs in 1893. It had four classrooms, each to accommodate 70 pupils. Rev. Lindsay was very popular with the young people. Perhaps they shared his liking for music and singing. Other people in the church and in the community certainly did. In March 1893, 50 members of the Free Church Musical Association gave a service of praise based on the story of Elijah, in the Church hall.

Appreciation of music and culture was not confined to church circles. In the following year, almost 100 Auchinairn School pupils performed the kinderspiel "Midshipmite". The Livingstone Literary Association also met in Auchinairn School, and the White Rose Lodge in Bishopbriggs. Auchinairn also had a Brass Band. Evening classes were held in Auchinairn School. The Cadder and District Literary and Dramatic Society were active, and the Cadder District Horticultural Show had taken place annually since 1862. In addition, the 8th Company of the 1st Lanark Artillery Volunteers was formed in Bishopbriggs.

After little more than three years at the church, however, Rev. Lindsay decided that it was time to move on. He was Inducted into Cathcart church in September 1895, and was succeeded at Bishopbriggs by Rev. R.W. Reid, a son of the manse. Rev. Reid was described as a man of deep fervour, and one who possessed a zest for life. His was a very busy ministry indeed. In addition to conducting regular services in his own pulpit, he conducted fortnightly services at Mavis Valley and Auchinairn. He was known for his works both in and outwith the church. It must have given him great satisfaction to be able to give a glowing report at the annual soiree on the work of his church and of the newly formed Dorcas Society, while Mr Armstrong spoke in like manner on the work and witness within the Sabbath School.

As the nineteenth century drew to a close, it would seem as though "Sleeping Hollow" was finally coming to life. Street lighting (albeit gas) was being provided and the district had been supplied with fresh Loch Katrine water. Bishopbriggs Church, as Cadder Free Church was popularly known, was flourishing. What would a new century bring?

Chapter 3
A new age dawns

The advent of the twentieth century may not have been greeted by the high powered acclamation reserved for the arrival of the Third Millennium one hundred years later. It was, however, welcomed with "High hopes" according to commentators and artists such as E.T. Paull (Dawn of the Century). Unfortunately tragedy struck almost at once, by way of an epidemic of influenza which had claimed many lives throughout the U.K. by the end of January 1900.

The Church nationally began the century on a high note. The Free Church and the United Presbyterian Church amalgamated to form the United Free Church. As a result of this union, the church in Springfield Road became known as Springfield United Free Church. The union was generally, but not unanimously, accepted by church members nationally and locally. Some Springfield members left later to establish a Free church at the foot of Auchinairn Road. It became part of the church which is generally referred to as the "Wee Free".

Rev. Reid remained as minister of Springfield church. He continued to witness well both in and out of the pulpit, and was in a position to give a good report on the work of the church at the annual soiree in March. Later in the year, a United Missionary service took place and was shared with Kenmure United Free Church (Kenmure had been part of the United Presbyterian Church until that year. Another shared event was a "Service of Sacred Song", where Springfield choir sang part of the service set to music. The first performance took place on a Friday evening at Springfield Church. This was followed by two further performances, one at the Mission Hall, Auchinairn, and the other at Kenmure U.F. Church.

In 1901 the growing district of Kenmure was annexed by Cadder Parish Council. This ensured that it would be part of Bishopbriggs in days to come. Auchinairn continued to thrive and in addition to the Mission hall, Bell's Hall was available for secular functions. Most significant event nationally that year was the death of Queen Victoria. Springfield Church continued to thrive and prosper through 1901 and 1902, under the leadership of Rev. Reid. At the annual soiree in 1903 he was in a position to report positively on the progress the church and of the Band of Hope, Sabbath School and Bible Class. Later that year, five pupils from the Minister's Bible Class were placed highly in the National Welfare of Youth Examinations. A considerable achievement.

Under Rev. Reid's leadership, the Kirk Session became involved in civic affairs. They presented a petition to the Lower Ward Committee against the annoyance caused by bus drivers on the Sabbath day, and against the obstruction created at the tram terminus. In those days trams did not turn into Kenmure Avenue but terminated on the main road, in front of the shopping area. 1904 came along. On the world stage, Mr Rolls teamed up with Mr Royce to make quality motor cars. This had no immediate impact on Springfield Church, but other events did. Rev. Reid's highly acclaimed book, *Mountains of the Bible, their Lessons for the Young* was published in January. That same month Ralston U.F., a church extension charge, unanimously elected Rev. Reid to be their minister. He rejected the call, and continued to work and witness in Bishopbriggs.

A special service was held in March to celebrate Rev. Reid's eighth anniversary at the church. Later that year, five new elders were ordained and six new deacons appointed to assist in the work of the church which was thriving and expanding. Where would it all end? Naturally, news of such a successful ministry was not confined to Auchinairn, Bishopbriggs and Mavis Valley. Word was getting around and in June of that year Rev. Reid was unanimously called to North Church, Dumfries. Springfield was sorry to see their minister go, but the call was sustained. It is interesting to note that a year later, this remarkable man had more that 160 young people in the Bible class of his new church. He died on 25 April 1954.

During the vacancy which followed Rev. Reid's departure to Dumfries, services were occasionally conducted by visiting preachers. One of them was Rev. Robert Gordon from Jacksontown, Michigan. Robert was brought up in Bishopbriggs before emigrating to the U.S.A. He had been baptised in Bishopbriggs/Springfield Church where his father served as church officer and elder. Robert's mother assisted her husband by preparing the church during the week. While so doing she would often pray that some day she might see and hear her son preach the gospel. Her prayers were fulfilled on 18 September 1904, when Robert led the morning service at Springfield Church. Sad to say, Mr Gordon senior, a miner, had been killed at work several years earlier.

Springfield Church was to remain vacant for the remainder of 1904.

Chapter 4
People of note

The Rev. Henry Taylor, M.A. was called to fill the vacancy at Springfield United Free Church. Like others before him, it was his first charge. He was elected on 8 February 1905 and ordained on 4 April that year. The only problem recorded during his early days was the poor state of Springfield Road. This was brought to the attention of the local authorities. On the plus side, the Cantata, "Saul of Tarsus" was performed by the choir on a Friday evening, shortly after Rev. Taylor arrived. During his ministry the choir became established formally as a church choir under the leadership of Mr S. Carslaw, precentor for many years.

After only nine months in office, Rev. Taylor was in a position to make a good report to the congregation at the annual social. 54 members had joined during that short period and the church was financially sound. There were problems, however. The union of the Free Church and the United Presbyterian Church in 1900 had not been welcomed by a number of Springfield members who, as previously mentioned, left to form a church of their own. A bitter dispute arose as to the ownership of the church in Springfield Road and its associated legacies. The dispute reached crisis point and much of Rev. Taylor's time and energy were devoted to resolving the matter. He succeeded in securing the Springfield Road building for the United Free Church but the Cleland bequest was lost. In 1906 the Government set up a Commission to deal with such disputes. It was a time of union nationally and a three way merger saw the United Methodist Church come into being.

Back in Bishopbriggs, Kenmure United Free congregation was also flourishing. They had commenced building a new church at Stuart Drive. It was, however, a sad time at Cadder Church, especially for the minister, Rev. Watt and his family. His second son, Nigel Graham Watt, a student at Glasgow University, was drowned while swimming with the Kelvinside Academy Cadet Corps. A memorial was installed at Kelvinside Academy in 1907. Returning to Springfield, despite the loss of the Cleland Bequest, the church became self supporting. Sad to say, Rev. Taylor decided to move on and was translated to a new charge in February 1908. He became colleague successor to Rev. J. McEwan at Sydney Place United Free Church, Glasgow. Two years later it was reported that 400 had joined that church since his arrival. He gave educational lectures during the winter months and was strong on Temperance.

By this time, Springfield Church was part of a growing and developing community. Glasgow tram cars had started running to Bishopbriggs in 1903, Stobhill Hospital opened in 1905, and Bishopbriggs Golf Club and Bishopbriggs Bowling Club were both established in 1906. It is hardly surprising, therefore, that there was considerable interest among ministers with regard to the vacancy created at Springfield Church. They preached in competition. One candidate was a Y.M.C.A. agent who had worked in India. On 1 June, however, the call went to Rev. Thomas Neilson B.D. He was ordained on 3 August 1908.

Rev. Neilson was a scholarly man and a fine preacher. He gave monthly lantern lectures on New Testament subjects in the Mission Hall at Auchinairn. Like his predecessor, he was strong on temperance and on 1 and 2 January 1909, Springfield Church held a Temperance Holiday in Kenmure Church hall, which stood at the centre of Bishopbriggs in those days. Rev. Neilson opened the proceedings on 1 January and one of the elders, Councillor J. Stirling, did so on the 2nd. Concerts, games, etc. were held throughout. 1 January 1909 was memorable for another reason. An Old Age Pension was paid for the first time, to those age 70 and over.

Rev. Neilson continued his dedicated ministry. A Flower Service was held in the church one September evening. Flowers and bulbs had been donated by members of the congregation. The choir sang appropriate anthems and Rev. Neilson preached a sermon on the text "Others cut down branches of trees and strewed them in the way". The flowers were later donated to Glasgow Royal Infirmary, Stobhill Hospital and the Sick Children's Hospital. About that time, two proposals relating to Bishopbriggs fell through. One was to run a tram service to Kirkintilloch, the other to widen and deepen the Forth and Clyde canal so that Battleships could pass through. Had the latter happened, Mavis Valley rather than Bishopbriggs may well have become the centre of the community. As it was, Mavis Valley had an active church at that time. It was also about then that the Glasgow Presbytery decided to "transport" Wellpark Church to Colston (now Colston Wellpark).

Rev. Neilson continued to work tirelessly through 1911 and into 1912. A sale of work was opened by Lady McInnes Shaw, and another Flower Show took place. In January 1913 Rev. W Lindsay, then with St Marks U.F. Church, Glasgow, Returned to Springfield to give a fund raising lecture. His subject was his visit to Canada. The following month, Councillor E. Rosslyn Mitchell, L.L.B. gave a lecture on Napoleon. In those days the Kirk Session was recognised as a court and in May of that year a church member, Daniel Redmond, published a certificate from Springfield Kirk Session indicating that they had examined him and found a fama against him to be untrue.

In 1914 war was declared. The work of the church continued and the Sabbath School outing that year was to Drumchapel, a village in those days. By all accounts, Rev. Neilson was working hard. Too hard it would seem. On 4 April 1915, he preached in St Stephen's Church, Glasgow. His text was John chapter 13, verse 19. Sad to say he took ill in the pulpit, and died that evening. On 1 November a memorial tablet to Rev. Neilson was unveiled by former

---

Footnote.
A FAMA was a prevalent report of scandalous or immoral behaviour. More serious would be a FAMA CLAMOSA which would be supported by the Kirk Session.

minister Rev. Lindsay, then minister at Chalmers Church, Edinburgh. His text, "The woman who broke the alabaster box of ointment". A large sum of money had been raised to provide the memorial, and the residue was used to purchase a small organ for use at Auchinairn Mission Hall.

So it was that Springfield United Free Church became vacant once more.

Chapter 5
Men of parts

"He was a man of parts" is a compliment seldom used today but it describes quite a number of men who graced the pulpit or were members of Springfield Church. The implication being that they were multi-talented. The Rev. Thomas Neilson B.D. was such a man. So also was the man who followed him. On 5 July 1915, Rev. Lewis A. Sutherland, M.A. was elected minister, and ordained on 2 September. He was, indeed, a man of many parts being outgoing and vivacious, a fine preacher, a soloist and a piper. He often played his pipes and led children on Sabbath School outings. In June of the following year, he married a Miss McLure, who supported him in his ministry. One of his earliest tasks was to attend a function at which the local farmers entertained 200 wounded soldiers from Stobhill Hospital.

Many Auchinairn and Bishopbriggs families were touched by the war. A roll of honour was maintained listing members of the parish with church connections who were serving their country. Sad to say, eleven of them did not return. Their names were listed on a memorial plaque which was attached to the front of the Communion Table and ceremoniously unveiled later. One family lost two sons, L/Cpl Thomas and Private William McClymont. Another sad loss, although not war related, was that of James A. Cuthbert, B.L. He died in August 1918. Mr Cuthbert, an office-bearer, was associated with all six previous ministers at the church. He served as Session Clerk, Clerk to the Deacons' Court, Foreign Mission Treasurer and Sabbath School Teacher.

Church life was different in those days. For example, members were expected to pay seat rent. This realised the sum of £25:7/ in 1917. Another difference is that the church operated a Poor Fund. Seven Bishopbriggs residents and ten Auchinairn residents benefited that year. One similarity with the present day was the ongoing necessity for repairs. On 14 September 1917 the church had to be closed just after morning service, due to a serious problem with the roof. (A similar thing happened to the same building, now the Springfield Hall, towards the end of 2004.) The church roof problem continued and in the 1930s Mr Kennedy of the Scottish Wire Rope company was consulted with a view to stabilising it by means of wire rope. On Mr Kennedy's advice, however, metal bars were subsequently installed, as the ropes would have created inward pressure making the walls likely to collapse.

Back in 1917, Kenmure Church agreed to Springfield congregation holding evening services in their church while repairs were carried out. At the same time, Auchinairn Hall was also in need of urgent attention. Small surprise that the church faced a projected deficit of £10 that year, and a church door collection was considered necessary. By the beginning of 1918 a credit balance of £6 was predicted. Although just making ends meet, the church did not neglect the needs of others. Eight retiring offerings were uplifted in the year. They were for the Poor fund, Youth of the church and education, Home Mission, Congregational Fund, Red Cross, Glasgow Hospitals, and the Central Fund, respectively. Locally, the church arranged for five hundred weight of coal to be delivered to six Bishopbriggs and ten Auchinairn residents, who were in need.

Back at the church there was trouble. The Church Officer resigned, but withdrew his resignation when assured that someone would be available to supervise the Sabbath School children prior to commencement of their meeting. Clearly children in those days were not so well behaved as we are led to believe they were. On the other hand, there may have been a more sinister reason for the resignation. Rodents frequented the premises and one Deacons Court minute clearly states - "Give the Church Officer rat poison".

There was a further departure in 1918, that of James K. Stirling who was called up for military service. Like others mentioned, he was a man of parts. Mr Stirling returned to serve church and community well. He became a J.P., as did two other members, Robert Brown of the Groves and Mr Stirling's brother, William. Back to 1918. It seemed to be a year for resignations. Rev. Lewis Sutherland had only been at Springfield Church for little over three years when he received a call from Brandon Street U.F. Church, Motherwell. Rev. Sutherland preached his last sermon at Auchinairn Hall. This was appropriate as he had always been interested in the mission there. His final sermon was on the text "Farewell" from Paul's Epistle to the Corinthians. Like several other former ministers, Rev. Sutherland remained on good terms with the congregation of Springfield Church, which he often referred to as his "First love".

Concern was expressed about the manse being vacant during the winter months, and letting was considered. Rather like what happened in 2004. As had occurred during previous vacancies, there were numerous applicants for the charge. One preached in February but it was not until June that a minister was called. He was Rev. J. Watson Kelly, an earnest and faithful witness and a fervent evangelist. During his time the church made a vain attempt to have the Home Mission Board fund an evangelist to conduct regular Sunday evening services at Auchinairn.

Auchinairn Hall was used for many purposes. One of the elders, Mr Linn, was given permission to use it during a local election. Mr Linn was also a man of parts, being a member and president of the bowling club among other things. There is a story about him. He and his family were travelling by train to Lenzie to look at a house they were thinking on buying. The train stopped at Bishopbriggs. The Linns looked out of the window and saw houses that had just been built in Ruskin Square. When they arrived at Lenzie, they crossed over to the other platform, took the next train back to Bishopbriggs, and bought a house in Ruskin Square. Their daughter, Ella, was a founder member of the original Springfield Badminton club.

Rev. Kelly only remained at Springfield Church for two years, so in 1921, the church was vacant again. What would happen next?

Chapter 6
Difficult times

Although the war, supposedly to end all wars, was over, Europe remained a troubled place. Mussolini founded the Italian Fascist Party, there was trouble in Ireland, and unemployment in Britain was over a million. Locally, however, life went on. It was proposed to create a golf course at Auchinairn and, in due course, Little Hill came into being. New houses were being built, and further recreational facilities were planned. Springfield Church had been gifted a new organ in 1920. The Junior Choir was doing well and the creation of a Juvenile Choir was to follow. The church was financially sound just then and good progress was being made.

It is hardly surprising, therefore, that there was considerable interest among the clergy when Springfield became vacant again, in 1921. One applicant was an experienced minister, Rev. Robert Primrose. His trial service was to prove a bit of a nightmare for him, however. He came straight from a yachting holiday on the Clyde, wearing ordinary clothes on the assumption that a preaching gown would be available at the church. Unfortunately, this was not so. The Session Clerk offered to lend the minister his coat but it would not fit, so Rev. Primrose had to preach in unecclestical clothes (unheard of in those days). He even had to borrow his son's breeches and his brother-in-law's frock coat for the evening service.

Under the circumstances, Rev. Primrose was most surprised when he received the call to be minister at Springfield Church. He differed from all other previous ministers of Springfield in that it was not his first charge. In fact, it was said of him that he had a long and varied experience, and a record of considerable service. He was also a holder of the Volunteer Decoration. His induction took place in September 1921.

About that time, Springfield founded a football team. It played in the Churches League (a league known for robust play and uncompromising tackles). The church later donated fifteen shillings toward the purchase of a Springburn and District Football Trophy. From a cultural point of view, a Social and Literary club for young men met every second Tuesday in the church hall. The vestry had recently been refurbished, and a girls' Bible class met there on Sunday afternoons. Further alterations being considered at that time were the roof to be properly repaired, a gallery erected and electric lighting installed. Returning to the vestry, it was proposed that a bottle of spirits be kept there, for medicinal purposes. The bottle disappeared but was replaced. The story goes that the bottle disappeared again and it was proposed that rather than replace it a couch be placed in the vestry for use in the event of illness in the church.

Sad to say, there was great hardship locally at that time, due to unemployment. A special collection was, therefore, held to boost the church benevolent fund. To make matters worse, foot and mouth disease struck locally, followed by Anthrax in 1924. On the bright side, the right-of-way between Auchinairn and Bishopbriggs was improved. Many Springfield Church members came from Auchinairn and used that route, later known as "The Back Road to Bishopbriggs". One who used it was a blind boy from Auchinairn. On a February Sunday in 1924, he walked alone through slush and snow to get to church.

Prior to this and despite the depression, in 1923 Springfield Church and Sabbath School hired a special train to take them to Campsie Glen for their annual outing. Several hundred attended. Bishopbriggs was quite a mix in those days. On the one hand there were several hundred unemployed. On the other hand, a visitor described it as a frolicsome place, with a bowling green, two golf courses, three tennis courts, four football pitches and two recreation grounds. In reality, times were hard. Those were growth years, however. The population of just over 3,000 in 1911, had more than doubled, to 6658, by 1931. Sad to say, there was a rough element living locally in those days and, on several occasions, church windows were broken. The church faced further expenses. The roof had not been repaired properly. There was a little money to spare, however, and thirty new cups were bought for social purposes, the old ones being sold to a dealer. Yet another change in tradition took place in December 1923 when the first ever wedding ceremony took place in the actual church. Hitherto, they had been held in the vestry.

1924 began with a cautious note being sounded. The Deacons Court asked the congregation to be more liberal in their givings, especially in the special monthly collections. Their caution was justified when it was found that a further £250 would be required to repair the church roof again. It was also felt that the time had come to build a new hall to seat 150. Tenders were invited, and Messrs. Cowieson offered to erect the new hall and repair the roof for £405. The church was up-beat at that time. Rev. Primrose presented the congregation with a new organ. At the annual social he was able to inform the meeting that 48 new members had joined the church. At the same meeting, however, the treasurer sounded a cautionary note on finances.

All in all, 1924 was a good year for the church. It took part in the 9th World Sabbath School Convention, which was held in Springburn Public Hall that year. (This hall still stands in 2005 but has been derelict for many years.) Sabbath Schools were well attended in those days, and a visiting preacher mentioned that he had attended Springfield Sabbath School himself, as a boy. Towards the end of the year, a lady by the name of Peggy Eason, sang "The Holy City" at the morning service. A report in the local newspaper mentions this but adds that the congregation did not applaud, as this would have been indecorous.

In 1925, the new hall was opened but funds were still required to pay for it. One who assisted was the Marquis of Graham. He gave a lecture entitled "Rambles round Europe" in aid of the fund. As an added attraction, local entrepreneur, Sir Hugh Reid, chaired the meeting. Sad to say, Rev. Primrose's health was failing. He intimated his intention to resign on medical grounds, but remained in office until September. At one of his last services, he gave thanks that the building had been redecorated and illuminated (electric lighting installed). He preached his farewell service on 3 October 1926. His text, John 12:32.

Many years later, Rev. Primrose's grandson, Bob Wilson played football for Arsenal and Scotland, before becoming a T.V. personality.

Chapter 7
Growth and reunion

1926 was the year of the General Strike. Hardship was experienced locally, mainly due to lack of employment. It was also a year when many trees were blown down and harvest damaged by heavy rain. Despite all this, progress was being made in Bishopbriggs. A new tennis club was founded. It was called Springfield. Its court was at the top of Springfield Road, a cul-de-sac in those days, and its first meeting took place in the church. Members blotted their copy book, however, by using too many lights, and one of them actually stood on a chair. That apart, the main concern of the church was to find a new minister. During the vacancy, a rather nice gesture took place. In 1897, an elder by the name of John Armstrong gifted Communion cups, flagon and trays to the church. John left several years later to become a founder member of the local Free Church. John's gift remained the property of Springfield church until 1927 when the elders agreed to hand those elements over to the Free church for their use.

Returning to the vacancy, there were numerous applicants, as previously. On this occasion, however, a lady recommended a minister she knew of. His name was Donald Martin, M.A. He preached, was elected unanimously, and his induction took place in February. Under Rev. Martin's leadership there was a bonding of congregation and community. There were problems, however, on one occasion a partly completed bird's nest had to be removed from the rope space on the Sunday morning to permit the Beadle to ring the bell. One of the birds escaped. The other remained in church until captured by a member who was also a Scottish rugby international. The bird was ejected but sat outside protesting throughout the service.

By 1928, the church had a Girls' Association, a Senior Bible Class, a Band of Hope at Springfield and Auchinairn, and Sabbath Schools meeting at both venues. An average of 122 young people met at Springfield on a Sunday morning, and 178 at Auchinairn. The following year, a ladies' group began to meet. This later became the Guild, which celebrated its 70th anniversary in 2000. 1929 was a momentous year in the history of the church in Scotland. Union between the United Free Church of Scotland and the Church of Scotland took place. It is said that 12,000 people gathered in Edinburgh to witness the "Union Assembly". The Moderator was Rev. Dr. John White. The Lord High Commissioner was the Duke of York (later King George VI). He agreed to enter by a side door to symbolise the separation of Church and State.

Back in Bishopbriggs, the last meeting of Springfield United Free Church took place on Friday 27 September, and the first meeting of Springfield Church of Scotland took place on 25 October. In the meantime, the Duchess of York (Best known in her later years as Queen Mother) passed through Bishopbriggs on 16 October. Church union was celebrated in fine style locally. Springfield Sunday School marched from the church to Johnstone Memorial Church Recreation Ground, which covered the area between Colston Wellpark church and Colston Road. There they met up with children from all the other Sunday Schools in Bishopbriggs and Springburn for an outdoor service. Close to 10000 adults and children attended. So it was that the 1920s ended on a high note from a church point of view. Nationally and internationally, however, troubled times lay ahead. The 1930s saw the rise of such people as Mosley and Hitler. At home, unemployment and hardship continued. Men were living rough. Over the course of one weekend, sixteen men were arrested for sleeping in the kilns at Cadder brickwork.

Meanwhile, the church was making good use of Auchinairn Hall. 216 meetings took place there in one year alone. The population of Auchinairn was increasing, and Springfield church again made unsuccessful representations to the Home Board for assistance in the work there. Rev. Martin, therefore, continued to conduct regular evangelical meetings there. 40 of the ladies who attended enjoyed an outing to Troon. It was uneventful, unlike a later church outing. Visiting speakers were welcomed at Auchinairn and at Springfield. One of them, Rev. Maxwell Dewar, gave a lantern lecture on the Passion Play at Ober-Ammergau. It would seem that he was not the only overseas traveller to visit Bishopbriggs in those days, as the Cadder minister had occasion to complain about foreign coins appearing in the weekly offering.

1931 was a particularly cold year. One Sunday in March, the organ froze. A piano was used while office-bearers defrosted the "Kist-o-Whistles", as the organ was often called, with buckets of hot water. The cold weather did not stop the Girls' Association from producing a drama, which realised £9, in aid of Foreign Missions. Another organisation which was active in the community at that time, was the Kenmure Park Men's Own. Its main purpose was to propagate the Gospel. About 70 young men attended regularly. In addition to its Sunday function it also ran Saturday night dances, football teams, pipe band and many other activities. It remained active for many years, and brings back fond memories to those who attended. Kenmure Men's Own was closed to make way for a development that never took place. The hall was dismantled and transported to Kilsyth, where it became Kilsyth Rangers Football Club pavilion.

Back to 1931. The year ended with a cold spell, so it was decided to hold the annual Sunday School rally, which had continued since 1929, indoors rather than outdoor from then on. 1933 saw the death of two remarkable Springfield members. One was Miss Pitcairn, who served the church for more that 40 years as Sunday Schoolteacher, member of women's groups, and member of the Deacons' Court. The other was former organist, Tommy Gibbs, who played football for Queens Park, Partick Thistle and Dunfermline Athletic, as goalkeeper. Perhaps it was in memory of Tommy that a stranger visited choir practice one evening. It was an owl. It perched on the bell tower and competed with the choir. A crowd gathered outside to witness the spectacle, and declared the owl a worthy winner. The owl wasn't the only one who could sing. The

Junior Choir performed an operetta that year.

There had been a rather cold start to 1933. On one occasion, the Deacons Court met huddled round the fire, rather that in their usual seating formation in the hall. The weather improved sufficiently for the Auchinairn Mission to enjoy an outing to Inveraray in April. On the way home, however, the bus ran off the road and stuck in a rut. The party began to walk, but the elderly were given a lift in a passing furniture van, while the young and fit walked the three miles to Tyndrum. By contrast with the cold winter, there was a heat wave during the summer, and doors were left open one Communion Sunday. Unheard of in those days. 1933 saw other innovations. The playing of badminton in the church hall was agreed and the inaugural meeting of Springfield swimming club took place there also. By the middle of the decade, things were progressing well at Springfield church but further changes and challenges lay ahead.

Chapter 8
Gathering clouds

By 1934, there was political unrest in Great Britain, and throughout Europe. Rev. Martin, a gentle person, was deeply concerned, and opposed to war. Springfield Church members were becoming politically aware, and took an interest in world affairs, especially from a Christian point of view. They had long supported Foreign Mission work and continued to do so by raising funds for a variety of projects. The Woman's Guild sponsored an illustrated lecture on Palestine, and a missionary from Calabar gave an address on her work there, at Auchinairn Hall, that year. It was also the year when a Bishopbriggs man by the name of George Younger, won a free flight on an aeroplane by virtue of success in a newspaper competition. Years later, George became a local Councillor. Younger Quadrant in Bishopbriggs is so named in his memory. He also served as a member of Springfield Cambridge Congregational Board, some time later.

It is interesting to note that a number of Springfield, and later Springfield Cambridge, members were and are involved in local politics. Their views on politics differed but all of them agreed that their faith and Christian commitment came first. The civic authority had changed. Until 1930, local affairs were administered by Cadder Parish Council. Thereafter, however, Bishopbriggs, Auchinairn etc. became part of the 9th District of Lanarkshire. This new authority continued and accelerated the upgrading of local housing. The village of Lochfaulds was demolished, and many of the older houses in Jellyhill and Mavis Valley had demolition orders placed on them also. The same happened later in Auchinairn.

Many of those who left the villages were rehoused in the new Springfield scheme, close to Springfield Church. Some time later, houses were built on the Back Road, half way between Auchinairn and Bishopbriggs. Many of the people thus rehoused, began to attend Springfield Church. Private houses were also being built. On one occasion a sign saying "Show House" was removed from outside one of the new bungalows and placed at the door of a condemned house on Jellyhill Tarryrow. The church welcomed new members but did not neglect its outreach to Auchinairn. Rev. Martin took the opportunity to emphasise the importance of this work when the Presbytery carried out its Quinquennial visit. His plea for assistance once again fell on deaf ears. This did not deter the people of Springfield. Not only did they continue to support outreach locally, they also contributed towards National Church Extension. The Girls' Association produced three plays to raise funds for this cause, and the Guild organised a Sale of Work, which was opened by Lady Stirling of Glorat.

It was in 1934 that the local Free Church called its first minister, Rev. J.T.

Robertson. When its members broke away from Springfield in the early years of the twentieth century, they had built a church of their own, which opened in 1911. During the years that followed, it was served by pulpit supply until the decision was taken to call a minister. By then, only three of the original members remained. Another interesting event connected indirectly to Springfield took place that year. Group Captain Primrose, son of the late Rev. Primrose, V.D., R.N.V.R., left the R.A.F., and was appointed Air Mail Adviser to the Post Office.

The following year saw some changes at Springfield Church. Discussions took place with a view to altering the time of morning worship from Noon to 11. 00 a.m. (There were always two services in those days.) Several meetings took place, there was a vote, and the compromise time of 11.30 a.m. agreed. While the anniversary service took place in February, as usual, special arrangements were made to celebrate the 70th anniversary of the opening of the church. 1935 was the King's Jubilee year. This was celebrated also, and a donation given to the Prince of Wales Benevolent Fund.

While progressing well under the kindly leadership of Rev. Martin, the Church also faced up to its social responsibilities. There was a proposal that golf courses be opened on Sundays. This was strongly opposed by Glasgow Presbytery and by Springfield Church. Another problem was lack of support for the Band of Hope leadership at both Auchinairn and Springfield. This gave rise to concern as the church had always attached great importance to working with the young people of the community. About that time, however, the Kirk Session received a letter from leaders of a boys' club with a membership in the region of fifty, saying that they would like to start a Boys' Brigade company at Springfield Church. The Session invited a representative of the club to meet with them. That representative was John Davie. The meeting was positive, and Mr Davie went away to put final arrangements in hand.

Meanwhile, a letter of protest was received from Kenmure Kirk Session. The basis of the protest was that they had a Boys' Brigade Company (182nd Glasgow) and that Mr Davie, his assistants, and most of the boys in the club had left the 182 following a dispute. Springfield Kirk Session gave the matter due consideration but decided to support Mr Davie's initiative. Arrangements were put in place and on 4 October 1935, affiliation papers were signed. (4 October is a significant date as it was on that day in 1883 that the Boys' Brigade was founded, by Sir William Alexander Smith.) So it was that the 268th Glasgow Company came into being. John Davie was appointed captain. He served for twelve years, then retired. Until the day he died, everyone referred to him as "Captain Davie". A junior organisation called the Life Boys was also founded. The leaders were Agnes Pollock and Adam Kennedy. Agnes later married Willie Smith who served the church as Session Clerk for many years.

On to 1936. There was trouble in Europe and unemployment at home. The year began rather sadly when the pulpit was draped in black to commemorate the death of King George V. One of Springfield's long serving members, Henry Teape, also died, having served the church for more than thirty years. It is said that things go in threes. In this case the third death was that of an Auchinairn man, Charles Brown. Charles was 101 when he died. He had been married three times, and had 33 children.

Returning to the church, an increase in membership, and loss through death and moving away from the district, made it necessary to appoint new elders. In those days, this was done by election. On this particular occasion, there were 23 candidates for five positions. Sad to say, some only got one vote. The same procedure was adopted when filling the post of Organist the following year. On that occasion, three candidates were invited to play in competition with one another. The winner was a Mr Robert Proven, with 101 votes to 20 and nine, respectively. At that time, a second-hand organ was gifted by an Edinburgh church. Springfield then gifted the existing organ to Trinity Possil Church. Back at Springfield, there was further trouble with the roof. It became obvious that radical repairs were necessary. In the end, it was agreed to seek a grant from the Baird Trust.

As the decade drew to a close, there was mounting tension in Europe. What impact would it have on the church?

Chapter 9
War years

1939 came. The Girls' Association ran a Scottish night in February and presented two plays in March. Both events were in aid of schemes of the church. It was noted that the Girls' Association had raised £271 over the previous eleven years. Despite the fact that "Storm Clouds" were gathering over Europe, church activities continued as usual, for a time at least. Rev. Martin was strongly opposed to war. On one occasion when conflict had been narrowly avoided, he gave thanks from the pulpit the following Sunday morning. It transpired, however, that there would not be "Peace in our Time" as Prime Minister Chamberlain had promised. On Sunday 3 September, Mr Chamberlain informed Parliament "This country is now at war. We are ready".

Just how ready we were is a point worthy of debate. Gas masks were issued, and had to be taken everywhere, even to church. Air raid shelters were being hastily built. The basement of the church was considered for this purpose, but would have had to be strengthened. Glasgow Presbytery advised all churches to mount a fire watch at night. Sandbags were obtained for the church, as was other fire-fighting equipment such as stirrup pumps, long handled scoops, rakes, and water buckets. Thus prepared, attempts were made to carry on life and church life as normal, or as near to normal as possible. It was agreed to celebrate the October Communion but it was left to each elder as to how he carried out the delivery of Communion cards during the blackout (no street lights to be lit, or lights shown at any window or door). The retiring collection that Communion Sunday was in aid of the Forces' Comfort Fund. This fund was to enable parcels to be sent to service men and women.

Bishopbriggs saw numerous changes at that time. A Church of Scotland Canteen was set up in the mission hall. It was staffed by local ladies, many of them church members. The canteen proved to be most popular with service men stationed at the Gun emplacements, Rushiehill, at the Balloon Barrage and at the R.A.F. camp, which is now Low Moss Prison. The Education Authority requested accommodation on church premises for one primary class. Another request for use of accommodation came from the Salvation Army. They were granted Auchinairn Hall twice weekly, provided they were willing to assume responsibility for the Blackout. That hall was also used for Fire Guard lectures. The Home Guard (Dad's Army) were given use of it too. Unfortunately, they caused damage for which they agreed to pay but said that the Church might not get any money until after the war.

There were other ways in which war impinged on the church. Time of morning worship was changed to 11.00 a.m., and there was a 3.00 p.m. service instead of an evening service during winter months. The Life Boys met on a Saturday afternoon instead of a week day evening. When their leader, Ruby

Younger, was called up for military service her mother ran the team, almost single-handed, for the duration. Three of 12 newly appointed Deacons were also called up for military service. Back at church, railings and gates in front of the premises were removed, the metal being used for the "War effort". There were some patriotic gestures among the members also. Mr J.K. Stirling, J.P., received a sum of money as a token for his 25 years service as Treasurer. He immediately donated his gift to the Forces' Comfort Fund.

As war continued, efforts were made to continue normal activities. A Garden Fete took place as usual in 1941. The following year, there was an envelope collection in aid of church funds. The Girls' Association held a flower and vegetable sale. This raised £13, again in aid of church funds. Later that year, an Airgram was received from Sulenkama Hospital, South Africa, mentioning the present occupant of the "Springfield Cot". This cot was gifted to the hospital by the Girls' Association. Main concern at home, however, continued to be the war. There was bad news and good news, Dunkirk, the fall of Singapore, El Alamein and the Battle of Britain. Battle of Britain Sunday was commemorated locally one Sunday during September 1943. The youth of the district were led to Springfield Church by the 268th pipe band, for a service conducted by Rev. Martin.

Sad to say, Rev. Martin was not spared to conduct many more services. He took ill during the early part of October, died on 22nd, his funeral took place on 27th and a Memorial Service was conducted on 31st. On the day of his funeral, six Springfield office-bearers acted as pallbearers. He was buried in Dean Cemetery, Edinburgh. Rev. Martin was sadly missed. It was said of him that he never said a foolish thing, nor could do an unwise one. His death cast gloom on church and community alike. Public and congregation subscribed towards three Communion Chairs which were presented to Springfield church in his memory.

Life had to continue. The church electoral roll was prepared, and a vacancy committee of 13 appointed towards the end of December. In January the church suffered a further loss through the death of Mr J.K. Stirling, J.P. Mr Stirling had been a Sunday Schoolteacher for 46 years, a President of both the Glasgow Sunday School Union and the North District Sunday School Union. He also conducted outdoor evangelical meetings at Jellyhill, Mavis Valley and Auchinairn. He was a Parish Councillor for many years, and co-founded the Mission Hall, which was used as a Forces Canteen during the war.

The vacancy committee was faced with a formidable task in trying to find a minister during 1944, when so many of them were serving in the forces. About that time, however, a former army chaplain, Rev. John Cameron, had resigned his charge in Rothesay, to enable a union to take place there. He preached and was called to Springfield Church. His Induction took place on 11th May 1944. One of his first tasks was to comply with a message from the King for "All people to offer prayer for the success of the Allied Nations most recent venture". His Majesty was referring to the D-Day landings, which took place on 6 June.

During the year that followed, Rev. Cameron settled in. This was not without difficulty. His furniture had to be transported from Rothesay. Locally, there were heating problems in the hall and in the church. An act of vandalism resulted in several Auchinairn Hall windows being broken. On the plus side, however, the Home Board finally agreed to a grant towards the upkeep of said hall. Finally the war drew to a close. Preparations to celebrate began. Huge bonfires were erected. Welcome home banners were prepared, each bearing the name of a service man or woman. Germany surrendered on 7 May. Japan did likewise on 14 August. The war was finally over, but what would the future hold for Springfield Church?

Chapter 10
Problems and opportunities

Rev. Donald Martin a kind and gentle man, was sadly missed. His successor, Rev. John Cameron, was inducted on 11th May 1944. One of his first duties was to preside over the 9th annual display of the 268 Boys' Brigade. He was in distinguished company that evening as one of the guests was Dr MacIntosh, a former rugby internationalist, and another was local resident, Jimmy Caskie, a Scottish international football player.

In November, Rev. Cameron attended an open meeting of the Girls' Association where mention was made of the girls presenting a second cot to Sulenkama hospital. This one was in memory of Rev. Donald Martin. The three Communion chairs placed in Springfield Church in his memory were later transferred to Springfield Cambridge where they are still in use. Another former minister of Springfield Church, Rev. Lewis Sutherland, was also honoured at that time. He received an O.B.E. in the 1945 New Year honours list.

Back at Springfield, Rev. Martin proved to be a hard act to follow, as the saying goes. He had been kind and gentle. Rev. Cameron, on the other hand, provided strong and resolute leadership. Unfortunately, this resulted in personality clashes with some of the elders, and one or two left the Session at that time. On the other hand, Rev. Cameron's leadership style was appreciated by the young people of the church, who responded well to it. Sunday Schools and the youth organisations continued to thrive. The church and its members of all ages celebrated victory in Europe, then victory in Japan. When hostilities finally ceased, those of the church's youth leaders and nine of its office-bearers who had been on active service, returned home, and took up church duties once again.

Victory of a different type was also celebrated in the church that year (1945). The 268 Boys' Brigade band won the Glasgow Battalion Piping Shield, and one of its members, Bill Martin, was solo champion. Bill was third the following year, but regained his title in 1947. He later became an elder of Springfield Cambridge church. Not all the young people were a credit to the district, however. Once again the windows of Auchinairn Hall were broken.

The congregation continued to show interest in the wider work of the church, both at home and abroad. "Christian Aid" was established by British and Irish churches to help refugees from Europe. The Guild showed a film on the rebuilding of Iona Cathedral. 1945 was also the year when the question of women elders was raised. Springfield Kirk Session voted against the proposal, as did the congregation by 55 votes to 17. Actually, all the Bishopbriggs churches voted against this proposal. The churches of Glasgow Presbytery voted against by 136 to 75. The ladies of the congregation were unperturbed, however, and continued to work and witness as usual.

Church life thus continued. John Davie retired as Boys' Brigade captain. His successor was Ronald Dalgarno. Unfortunately, there was a slight altercation between him and the church officer. It was easily resolved but to avoid future misunderstandings, a Hall Committee was formed. By this time, the large hall was in a dangerous condition, and organisations such as the Girls' Association had to meet in the small hall. The youth organisations finally got together and sent a letter to the Kirk Session, proposing that a new hall be built. This was taken on board. The necessary representations were made and, in 1947, a delegation from Glasgow Presbytery arrived. They suggested that pews be removed from the sanctuary and that the church become a hall/church. Their attitude changed completely, however, when it was pointed out that all work would be undertaken by voluntary labour, and that the total cost would be £8500.

Prior to making a final decision on this project, the church was faced with two further problems, woodlice in the Manse and structural damage to the belfry. Unfortunately, the weight of bell and belfry was such that the roof was in danger of caving in. It was agreed, therefore, to sell the bell and demolish the belfry. Another object removed from the church at that time was the sounding board, which was positioned above the pulpit. Its purpose was to project the preacher's voice to the back of the church. It had been crafted sixty years previously by Robert Morrison, a former Beadle, and positioned by him and Harry Tainch of Myriemailing Farm. Many of the present church members live in houses on what were Harry's fields and farm buildings.

Returning to the question of the proposed new hall, the congregation met on 12th October 1947, to make a final decision. There was some debate and it became evident that opinion was divided, mainly on cost. It was then that Mrs Chalmers rose to say that with our faith we would surely find that the resources would be forthcoming, and proposed that the Hall Scheme be proceeded with. Her motion was seconded by Mr James McGeachie, and carried. The year prior to this event, Mr and Mrs Chalmers had donated a stained glass window to the church in memory of their three children who had predeceased them. When Springfield Cambridge church was built the window was transferred to the Cambridge chapel, and a light placed behind it. Mr Chalmers, an elder, died in 1950, but Mrs Chalmers remained an active church member for many more years.

Sad to say, the Girls' Association found it necessary to disband in 1947. The Boys' Brigade, on the other hand, went from strength to strength and, among other things, won the Piping Shield for the third time in succession. 1947 was quite a year locally. Mr Briggs, the then church officer, lived in Callieburn Road. He kept hens in an enclosure opposite his house. On looking out of his house one dark, snowy morning, he saw a large dark patch on the snow. He crossed the road and placed a bucket containing food for his hens on the dark patch. The bucked dropped several hundred feet, down an old mine shaft which had subsided during the night. Sad to say, he never saw bucket or hens again.

The same year saw significant changes locally. A compulsory purchase order resulted in 10. 83 acres of Springfield Farm being obtained for house building. Clearly, the population of the parish was about to increase. About the same time, a new church came into existence. On 12th September, Balornock North Church met for the first time in Auchinairn Co-operative hall. 1947 also saw the death of an outstanding local church woman, Miss Annie Armstrong. She became a Sunday School teacher at Springfield, which was then Bishopbriggs Free Church, in 1882, but left after the reunion of 1900 to become a founder member of the Free Church in Auchinairn Road. She actually started the Sunday School there, with a class of four little girls. Her first lesson was "Our Dwelling Place" from psalm 90.

Returning to Springfield. In 1949, one of the Boys' Brigade ex-members, Bobby Galloway, played football for Scotland against England in an amateur international at Hampden one Saturday afternoon. Next day, he attended B.B. Bible class. Bobby did this on each occasion in which he played in a home international. His gesture was greatly appreciated by staff and boys of the company. As the decade drew to an end, one wondered what the 1950s would bring.

Chapter 11
Ups and downs

So far as Springfield Church was concerned, the foundations for the 1950s were laid in the late 1940s. One in particular on 21 August 1948. It was then that Mr W. Douglas, Secretary of the Ferguson Bequest, laid the foundation stone for the new hall. The hall was later known as the Cameron Hall, named after Rev. Cameron who was minister at that time. Coins, newspapers of the day and the names of 39 volunteers who had worked on the hall, were placed under the foundation stone. Members of the congregation, and some non-members also, continued to work on the building of the hall. Although those thus employed worked well together there was friction in other aspects of congregational life at that time. The result was that one or two of the elders and several members left then, for a variety of reasons. Sad to say, two long

Laying of Cameron Hall foundation stone.

serving members of the congregation died about that time. One was Mr Chalmers, and the other Mr D. Lindsay. Mr Lindsay had been water-board engineer form many years, and several generations knew him as "Dan Lindsay, the Water Man".

A third death occurred in the congregation. That of 17 year old John MacKinnon, a member of the Boys' Brigade. Thereafter, John's parents donated an annual prize to the 268 B.B. boy who did best in the Bible Knowledge exam. Subsequent generations of 268 boys are well aware of the MacKinnon Award but may not know of its origin. On a brighter note, the new hall was finally completed at a cost of £7000, including seating. It was opened on Saturday 25 March 1950, by Professor J.G. Riddell D.D. Those who worked on the building of the hall, and those who supported them, were justly proud of their achievement. In those days, the hall had a platform. Curtains were provided and stage lighting installed. Great use was made of the hall for weekday and Sunday activities, and for many stage shows during the years that followed.

Further changes relating to the church were considered. One proposal was to sell the manse. Application for permission to do so was made to the 1951 General Assembly. The Assembly agreed but the title deeds for the ground clearly stated that it was to be used as a manse "for all time to come". Repairs, therefore, had to be carried out and the manse retained. On the other hand, permission to sell Auchinairn Hall was finally granted. Again, however, there were complications and some time elapsed before this intent could be carried out.

In September of that year, Rev. Cameron intimated that he would be resigning in the near future, as he and his family intended to emigrate to Canada. Mr Cameron demitted office on 30 January 1952, to take up an appointment as minister in New Brunswick, Canada. He did not lose interest in Springfield church, however, and made contact from time to time in the years that lay ahead. It was he who called it the "wee grey church" on account of its external appearance.

Once again Springfield church was without a minister, and in considerable debt. What would the future hold for the Wee Grey Church?

Chapter 12
Downs and ups

The Boys' Brigade once sang a song at a show. It began with the words, "We've all been having our ups and downs", and ended "Soon we'll be finished with ups and downs, and start on the downs and ups". The congregation of Springfield church was on a down during the early months of 1952. Granted, the new hall was proving a boon to the organisations but the church, once again without a minister, was confronted by a number of problems.

Repairs were required at church, manse and Auchinairn Hall. Loans had to be serviced. There were problems in relation to heating of both hall and church. Membership had decreased and showed no sign of increasing. A commentator called "Worker" wrote to the local newspaper saying how unhappy he was, having sat under all ten ministers of the church, and now finding such treasures as the Sounding Board and the Roll of Honour missing.

It was depressing to see Springfield at such a low ebb when the Church of Scotland was on the increase nationally and the population of Bishopbriggs rising. Things were not all gloom and doom, however. Following an inaugural meeting on 17 May 1950, a badminton club had been formed. By the time of the A.G.M. in 1952, there was a full complement of 40 members and a waiting list of 20. The club joined the Glasgow and District Badminton Association, began to play in the seventh Division, and had been promoted to the fourth Division by 1955.

Agreement was finally reached to sell Auchinairn Hall. It was eventually sold for £200. From a financial point of view, the Boys' Brigade embarked on a fund raising exploit. They gathered wastepaper and sold it to a pulp mill. The paper was stored in the manse wash-house during the vacancy. Other fund raising projects followed. The Badminton Club sponsored a play in April. Miss Bunty Pullar's dance class mounted a review over two evenings in aid of church funds. It was a great success and was repeated the following year. So it transpired that, despite a lengthy vacancy, the church was beginning to rally at last.

The vacancy committee were not exactly inundated with applications. One who did apply, however, was the assistant minister at High Carntyne, Rev. H.J. French. The committee heard him one Sunday and recommended that he preach as sole nominee. This he did on 7 September 1952. Those present at the service were astonished at his appearance. He stood 6'3" and weighed 19 stone. It was his warmth and sincerity, however, that endeared him to all the congregation. He was elected unanimously that very day.

Had Springfield church indeed finished with ups and downs, to start on the downs and ups?

Chapter 13
Onwards and upwards

It did not take Rev. French long to get his feet under the table. He quickly got to know the congregation and many others besides. At first he travelled everywhere on foot or by public transport. He would stop people and if they were new to the district he would inform them as to where Springfield church was and when Sunday services were held. If he met up with or heard of newcomers with a church or youth work background, he would make a point of visiting them. On such occasions, his parting words would generally be - "See you on Sunday". He was popular with young and old alike, and took a genuine interest in the community. An example of this was his acceptance of an invitation to be visiting speaker at a Kenmure Men's Own meeting on the first Sunday in January 1953. At the annual congregational meeting that year it was reported that there had been a marked increase in weekly offerings. One person who was very pleased to learn of the upturn of work and witness at the church was the visiting speaker, none other than Rev. Lewis Sutherland, D.D., O.B.E.

Another who was pleased with recent development at Springfield was "Worker". In an article in the local press, he suggested that the church spend some of its new found wealth in replacing the bell which had been sold for £20 in 1950. Unfortunately, this was not possible due to problems with the roof, which had caused the bell to be removed in the first place. "Worker" in the same article, recounted an incident which must have taken place many years ago. The Liberal Candidate had been successful in an election. Still celebrating, some of his supporters passed the church about 2.00 a.m. the following morning. They decided to ring the church bell and did so, much to the annoyance of the locals who lived "Up the Cottages". As that part of the district was then known. In those days the bell rope ran down the outside of the building, an anomaly which was rectified soon after.

Returning to 1953. Sunday School had greatly increased in numbers, and presented the church with a Pulpit Bible. 13 new members joined the church just prior to the June Communion. The interesting fact is that five of them were Boys' Brigade boys. The Brigade blotted its copy book soon after, however, and had to be reprimanded for storing drum kits in the ladies' toilet. Nothing daunted, the boys went off to Summer camp at Leven that year. Four of them formed what turned out to be a prize-winning quartet. They were James Houston, Billy Semple, Willie Forrest and David Wilson (yes, the same David Wilson who years later became Proprietor of Peat Inn).

Back at Springfield it was felt that the time had come to form an organisation for girls. Several ladies were consulted, and a Girls' Guildry company was formed. Mrs Meek became Honorary Guardian. Guardian was Miss Robertson.

The Guildry later became the Girls' Brigade. 1953 was, of course, Coronation year. Church and organisations took part in the many celebrations which marked the crowning of Queen Elizabeth II. Some nationalists in Scotland resented the "II" and several pillar boxes so inscribed, were blown-up. As the year drew to a close three magnificent stained glass windows were installed in the church behind the pulpit. They still exist in the twenty-first century but, sad to say, are now hidden from view behind the back wall of the stage in what is now Springfield Hall but was then the church. 302 people attended Communion in October of that year. A record at the time, which was soon to be broken not once but many times.

1954 had its ups and downs. Down came part of the garden wall at the back of the manse but it was soon repaired. Up went the number of people attending church and joining. One of the reasons for this was the hard work carried out by Rev. French and his supporters. Another reason was that many people attended Billy Graham crusades, which were being held at that time, made a decision to follow Christ and were encouraged to join their local church. Locally, the Girls' Guildry were warmly congratulated on their first annual display. Two of the Boys' Brigade boys, William Forrest and David Wilson, attended the first ever Boys' Brigade International camp at Eton. They presented the church with a commemorative Bible on their return. That year also saw the death of Rev. Dr. Lewis Sutherland, O.B.E. His mother was a direct descendant of William Knox, brother of John Knox, Scotland's greatest reformer.

January 1955 was a cold month, especially at Springfield Church. It was discovered early one Sunday that the heating system had broken down and could not be fixed in time for morning service. Nothing daunted, Rev. French made several telephone calls. As a result, when the congregation arrived some time later, there was a bus waiting to ferry them to Kenmure Men's Own Hall, which had been opened and heated, just for them. At the Annual Congregational Meeting that year, it was announced that membership was up by 97, and that there had been 42 baptisms, 15 weddings and 37 funerals during the year. In addition to all the usual activities, the church had a chess club and a country dance class at that time.

In September of that year, William Smith was appointed Session Clerk, Pro Temp. Pro Temp means for the time being, but Willie was to remain Session Clerk for many, many years. He became an expert on church law, presumably by studying *Practices and Procedures in the Kirk Session and Financial Boards* by Cox. A copy of this book had been purchased by the Deacons' Court in 1948 and was, hopefully, updated from time to time. As it was the 90th anniversary of Springfield, another publication appeared. This was a history of the church, written by William Stirling J.P., a former elder.

A further change took place that year. Ronald Dalgarno, resigned as Boys' Brigade captain, on health grounds. He was succeeded by James McGeachie, who later served the church as Elder, Presbytery Elder and Treasurer. Another interesting aside is that the Church Officer at that time was a woman, Mrs Sime. She was a cheerful soul, except on the mornings when the church boiler

B.B. camp, Filey. Rev. H.J. French in attendance.

refused to light for her. Her son, Hector, also became an elder and B.B. officer at a later date. Back in the fifties, the then treasurer must have been a happy man as the church had to buy more and bigger offering baskets at that time. Another happy man was Rev. French. He was invited to represent the former pupils at his old school's sports day. Weighing 19 stone it is hardly surprising that he was selected to be anchor man in the tug-o-war team. Talking of surprises, a burglar entered the manse one day. He was confronted and rather easily apprehended by the minister who, in addition to his height and weight, just happened to be a former Military Policeman.

1957 saw several changes at Springfield. The Boys' Brigade Company were presented with Colours for the first time. The church obtained a Visitors' Book, and Mrs Meek became leader of the Young Worshippers' League. This was an "organisation" for children who attended church instead of, or in addition to, Sunday School etc. Their attendance was recorded and they received an annual prize. 1957 was also the year when Bearyards farm was finally demolished. The original Free Church had met in the barn of that farm back in 1843. Some stones were collected from the farm to be made into a cairn and placed in front of the church. Sad to say, the cairn is long gone. Although rightly proud of its history, the church was, and is, forward looking also. It was agreed that a parish visitation should take place. That great evangelist, D.P. Thomson, visited Springfield in connection with this venture. D.P. was friend and confidant of Eric Liddell, Scotland's greatest athlete, himself a missionary and evangelist. One group which took part in the visitation was the newly formed Youth Fellowship. The venture was a huge success, and as a result, more people joined the church.

It is interesting to note that at that time, several members of the congregation were also interested in politics. One of them, James Young, became first Provost of Bishopbriggs, while Abie Vaughn and Ian McBryde were among the first elected members of Strathkelvin District Council. As the decade drew to a close, a week of socials was held at the church, primarily to enable old and new members to get to know one another. A Stewardship Campaign took place the following year, and the Minister set up a new record by baptising eleven babies one Sunday morning.

What would the 1960s hold for this, now vibrant, church?

Chapter 14
Triumph and tragedy

1960 was the 400th anniversary of the Reformation in Scotland. For this reason, October Communion at Springfield church was delayed by one week to the ninth. It turned out to be a memorable occasion. 413 members and 13 visitors took part, a record for the church at that time. Principal Mauchlin, D.D., friend and mentor of Rev. French, presided that day. At the Principal's invitation, Springfield church became corporate member of the Society of Friends of Trinity College. Trinity was the Glasgow college where ministers were trained in those days. It was in 1960, the then Prime Minister, Harold MacMillan, delivered his "Wind of Change" speech. He was referring to Africa, but could equally have been speaking of the world in general and Bishopbriggs in particular. Yuri Gagarin became first man in space, in 1961 and nine years later the first man landed on the moon.

Back on earth, the population of Bishopbriggs more than doubled during the decade to 21,684 in 1971. Political changes also took place and Bishopbriggs became a burgh, the Burgh Council first meeting on 5 June 1964. Springfield church rose to the challenge of this vast increase in local population. Just how well the church was doing was demonstrated at the Annual Congregational Meeting that year. Rev. French was in a position to report that membership had risen from under 400 in 1952 to 663 in 1961. During the same period the number of children in Sunday School had risen from 173 to 356. From a financial point of view the loan fund had closed in 1961 and the church was meeting all its contributions to the Church of Scotland for the first time.

Springfield did not sit back, however, but continued to work and witness vigorously under the leadership of its admirable minister. Both adult and especially youth organisations continued to grow to such an extent that at the next Annual Meeting, one of the youth leaders asked if consideration had been given to extending the premises. Rev. French replied that this was so, but that he would like to see a further rise in offerings. In April of that year, the Deacons' Court gave consideration to purchasing ground behind the church. At the same time, the Minister and five office-bearers attended a weekend course on Stewardship. This resulted in a Stewardship Campaign during the months that followed.

The spiritual life of the church was not neglected, and the number attending October Communion exceeded 500 for the first time in the history of the church. At the Annual Meeting in 1963 it was reported that membership was in excess of 800. Youth organisations continued to grow and the Youth Fellowship agreed to organise a visitation to the new houses in Woodhill estate on behalf of the church.

Changes were taking place. Miss Robertson retired as Guildry Guardian and was replaced by Miss Margaret Lawrie, who had grown up in the church. Other examples of leadership thus provided were Billy Semple who became Boys' Brigade captain, and Robert Lawrie, Leader in Charge of the Life Boys. Accommodation was tight, to say the least, especially on Sunday mornings and no sign of relief. That is, until an anonymous donation of £1000 was received for the building of new premises. Thus encouraged, the Deacons' Court signed missives for the ground in question that September. About the same time, a Young Wives' group was founded. Clearly Springfield church was really going places. Then tragedy struck.

Rev. H.J. French died suddenly on 31 October 1963.

Chapter 15
Moving forward

Rev. Henry J. French was sadly missed by all who knew him. Springfield church realised, however, that life must go on. It was 1963, so perhaps they were inspired by the words of Martin Luther King - "I have a dream". Could some of the dreams outlined by Rev. French become reality? Rev. J. Stewart was appointed Interim Moderator and Rev. Dr McCardil was the Locum. Both were remarkable men. Rev. Stewart having been born and brought up in Springburn and being long time minister of Colston Milton church, was well known to many of the older members. His kindly but firm leadership was just what the congregation required to move forward at such a time. Dr McCardil, a retired minister, was an inspirational preacher and dedicated pastor. Rather than take the direct route to the vestry on a Sunday morning, he would walk through the hall, stopping to speak to children and teachers in the Sunday School. On one occasion, at the end of a service, he ordered that the church doors remain closed. He then informed the congregation that two more Sunday School teachers were required and that the church doors would remain closed until this matter was rectified. He did not have long to wait for his two volunteers.

A vacancy committee of 19 was duly elected and went about the task of finding a new minister. Meanwhile, the church did not standstill. It was estimated that the new hall would cost in the region of £6,500, so fund raising began. The choir staged a concert in February 1964. A fund raising cruise on Loch Lomond was proposed, and greeted with enthusiasm. Tenders were requested and planning permission obtained.

Meanwhile, the vacancy committee were busy. They visited a number of churches to hear various preachers. They were most impressed by the then minister of New Stevenston church, Ayrshire, the Rev. David Hebenton, B.D. He was invited to preach as sole nominee on 15 May and was duly elected. His voice sounded vaguely familiar, especially to some of the men of the congregation. This was hardly surprising as "David Hebenton" read the football results on B.B.C. radio every Saturday evening. Needless to say he proved to be a most articulate preacher. His Induction took place in September that year. Soon after, he Baptised 13 babies one Sunday morning.

By this time, Bishopbriggs had aspired to Burgh status. First meeting of the Council took place on 5 June 1964. As previously mentioned, A Springfield elder, James Young, was elect to the office of Provost. Church membership continued to increase, and two morning services had to be held. One was at 10.15 a.m., the other commenced at 11.30 a.m., followed by Junior Sunday School at 1.00 p.m. Fortunately, tenders had been received for the new hall, which would cost £7,000. Building started early in 1965, and progress was good. So much so that the Congregational Board was able to hold their June meeting in Room 3 of the new premises. This room was lost when the new church was built. Part of it is now the vestry. The Boys' Brigade hut was also lost when the new church was built. This hut had originally been Dr. Miller's surgery. When he moved into new premises in February 1965, he donated the hut to the Boys' Brigade, provided they remove it. This was done early one Sunday morning, as that was the only time which the police would agree to such a precarious load being transported through the streets of Bishopbriggs.

Such enterprise was all very well but it did not solve the basic problem. The church itself was too small. Something had to be done. Finally the Church Extension Committee agreed to a larger church being built, but how could this possibly be brought about. Did someone have something in mind? Yes! Someone did. More later. It was 1965, Springfield's centenary year. Rev. Andrew Herron was guest speaker at the Centenary Gathering held on Friday, 8 October. Centenary Communion was celebrated on the 10th. On that occasion, Rev. Hebenton was assisted by Rev. Samuel McGeachie, a member

Rev. Hebenton and office-bearers.

of a family which had a long connection with Springfield Church. Over 600 people took part in that Communion.

Springfield was not prepared to rest on its laurels. A congregational visit was put in hand early in 1966. A Men's Association was considered, and came into being. One of the church members, Mrs Gregson, started an organisation for boys under Life Boy age. It was called the "Shipmates" and is now known as the "Anchor Boys". Later, Mrs Gregson resumed her studies, became a Primary School teacher, and later still she became Rev. Gregson, B.A., B.D.

On 30 October 1966, Principal Mauchline dedicated the new hall to the memory of the late Rev. H.J. French. He also dedicated a lectern which now stands in the new church. A new organ was installed later that year. This meant that the old pipe organ was no longer required. It was dismantled, not too ceremoniously, by Rev. Hebenton and some of his office bearers, early in 1967. So ended the "Kist-o-Whistles".

That year began well and once again the Communion attendance record was broken, 697 members and 12 visitors taking part. A garden Fete was held in May. In June, however, to the surprise of the congregation, Rev. Hebenton announced his intent to demit his charge and undertake teacher training. He did so in October. Once again Springfield church was vacant. Rev. Gourlay Black, a retired minister, was appointed locum. During the months that followed, he proved to be a fine pastor and an excellent preacher. In March 1968, a letter was received from the fore-mentioned Rev. Andrew Herron, Clerk to the Presbytery of Glasgow, outlining possible union with Cambridge Street Church. A union which would result in funds being realised with which to build a new church.

Chapter 16
Basis of union

By the beginning of 1968, Springfield Church was virtually bursting at the seams. Attendance at Communion was verging on the 700 mark, and there were over 600 children attending Sunday School. Clearly, something had to be done. The fore-mentioned letter from the Clerk to the Presbytery of Glasgow was received, read and given careful and prayerful consideration. However, in view of the overcrowding even the slightest hesitation in accepting the offer of funds with which to build a new church may seem surprising. The reason for the hesitation was that until then Springfield Church with its Free Church background had always exercised its hard won right to call a minister of its own choosing. This would not be possible, however, as Cambridge Street Church had stipulated that the united church must accept their minister, Rev. James Cran, as minister of the united charge.

Let us, at this point, make brief reference to the history of Cambridge Street Church. During the 1830s houses were being built in and around the Port Dundas, Garnockhill and Cowcaddens area of Glasgow. Among those who moved into the new houses were members of the Secession Church. A group of them got together on 19 December 1833 and resolved to build a church. A committee was formed, a site obtained at 156 Cambridge Street and the building was ready to be occupied by November 1834. Its members petitioned the Presbytery of the United Presbyterian Church, and a congregation was formed in May 1834. A Mr John Eadie was appointed to perform pulpit supply. The congregation, now numbering 98, were so impressed with Mr Eadie that they decided to call him to be their full-time minister. He accepted, and was ordained on 14 September 1835.

Two years later and there were 400 members. The church was too small, and had to be extended in 1846. By 1861 there were 1,000 members. In November of that year Lansdowne Church was built. There is a poem which may apply to it-

> This church was built for Doctor Eadie;
> It is not for the poor and needy.
> The rich come here and take their seat;
> The poor can go to Cambridge Street.

Second minister of Cambridge Street was Rev. Robert Cameron. He was inducted in October 1864. The church continued to thrive and, in 1868 it was re-seated. Outreach continued and in 1881-82 a Mission Hall was built in Sawmillfield Street. Unfortunately, Rev. Cameron's health began to fail, and he resigned in November 1897, dying in April the following year. Rev. Peter

Smith was called in 1898. In 1900 Cambridge Street Church, like Springfield, became part of the United Free Church. Rev. Smith continued to minister at Cambridge Street until he retired in May 1926. He was followed by. Rev. William Main Reid in 1926; Rev. Robert Black Kincaid in 1938; Rev. James MacArthur Ewing in 1947 and Rev. James Cran in 1954.

The period following the Second World War saw a dramatic decline in the number of people living in and around Cambridge Street. Some who left to live elsewhere continued to attend their old church for a while, but the congregation dwindled. The city centre was being redeveloped on business and commercial grounds and land was at a premium. Finally, Glasgow Corporation placed a compulsory purchase order on Cambridge Street Church building. It was at this time that proposals for union were presented to the congregation by the Presbytery of Glasgow. The Cambridge Street folk agreed to the proposed union with Springfield Church but insisted that Rev. Cran be minister of the united charge. This was agreed. The final act of worship, a Communion service, took place in Cambridge Street on October 1968. The building was demolished in 1969.

Meanwhile, the basis of union had been agreed at a meeting of the Springfield Congregation on 5 June 1968, and Rev. James Cran became first minister of Springfield Cambridge Church.

Chapter 17
Union and progress

The official union between Springfield and Cambridge Street churches took place on Thursday 5 September 1968. Springfield Cambridge Kirk Session first met on 1 October. The Session were pleased to see how quickly their new minister had settled in and got down to the work of church and parish. It was noted that he visited patients in Stobhill Hospital every Monday morning, that he had started visiting each district in the company of its elder, and that he had arranged to meet leaders of the various Sunday School departments. As Rev. Cran did not have a car, he carried out all his business and visitations on foot. In this way he quickly got to know the district, and the people of Bishopbriggs soon got to know him. He had a friendly greeting and a ready smile for everyone. He almost invariably began his sermon with the words - "My dear friends". First Communion to be celebrated by the united congregation took place on 6 October at 10.00 a.m., 11.45 a.m. and 6.30 p.m. A total of 712 members and 2 visitors took part that day.

Changes were taking place locally at that time. Bishopbriggs was to become a smokeless zone by the end of the following year. With this in mind, the Congregational Board agreed to install two new electric fires in the manse. This is clearly minuted. Not so clear is the meaning of the minute which states that - "A drain behind the Cameron Hall has silted up, and Mr Archibald is looking into the matter". Mr Archibald, Property Convener at the time, was yet another elder who was a member of the Burgh Council. By then it was recognised that the church required several new elders. Six were nominated, and became the first new elders of Springfield Cambridge Church. At the same time it was proposed that consideration be given to the appointment of women elders at the next Kirk Session meeting.

The Kirk Session met in January 1969, but agreed not to admit women elders. At that same meeting it was noted that there were 1484 members on the roll. In addition, it was reported at the March meeting that there were 135 children in the Young Worshippers' League. It was a good year for the church. The six new elders were ordained, the last ordination to take place in the old building. All youth and adult organisations continued to function and prosper throughout 1969. Mrs Cuthbert succeeded Miss Lawrie as Guildry Guardian, and Mr Stewart replaced Mr Reynolds as roll keeper of the Young Worshippers' League. Glasgow Presbytery chose Springfield Cambridge as the venue for a Sunday School Teacher Training course. Unfortunately, expected progress with the new church building did not materialise.

By contrast, the work of the congregation made good progress. The Boys' Brigade company produced their annual show and pantomime, which ran for three nights during November. In the same month, the Men's Association, now one of the largest in the country, had Mr Marshall J. Harris, National Officer of the United Nations Association, talk to them on Human Rights. The Men's Association was particularly strong nationally at that time. This was reflected in that 500 members attended the Glasgow Association annual service at Adelade Place Church in November that year. Sad to say, the old Cambridge Street building was destroyed by fire about that time. There was still no progress with the new building due to access problems and other factors. Legal advice was taken towards the end of the year.

1970 was a significant year in the history of all Christian Churches. It saw the publication of the New English Bible. Back at Springfield Cambridge, noting that there were over 1400 members on the roll, the Home Board decided that it was time find a Lay Missionary to act as Assistant Minister. Mr Elliot was appointed in May. The Boys' Brigade company went overseas for the first time that year and camped at Port Rush in Northern Ireland. They had a distinguished visitor one day. It was Bertie Peacock, former Celtic and Northern Ireland football star. He spoke to the boys on the importance of team work in all aspects of life. It seemed to work as the boys won several competitions later that year, including the Glasgow Battalion Cross Country championship.

Finally, there was a break through in the building of the new church. Messrs. Varney proceeded with final drawings for the building, the first church using metric measurements. There were, however, two problems. The choir were unhappy with the proposal that they be situated on a balcony at right angles to the pulpit. This was altered. Second problem was insufficient car parking facilities to meet with Local Authority regulations, so the Boys' Brigade hut had to be demolished prior to work commencing. Room three of the Henry J. French Hall was also lost. Meanwhile, 300 members of the congregation had a most enjoyable sail on board the *Sir Walter Scott* on Loch Katrine.

Back home, all was finally ready, and the laying of the new church foundation stone arranged for 5 June 1971. Rt. Rev. Andrew Herron was Moderator of the General Assembly of the Church of Scotland at that time. As he had been the architect of the Springfield and Cambridge Street Church union, he was invited to lay the foundation stone of the new church building. Since this was the first occasion on which a Moderator had visited Bishopbriggs, Rt. Rev. Herron was received by Provost Proctor and members of the Council in the Burgh Chambers at 2.15 p.m., prior to the stone-laying ceremony at 3.00 p.m. Altogether, it was a momentous occasion. Once again, however, the congregation did not rest on its laurels. A Parish Visitation committee was set up. Nor was there compromise in witness. Although keen to gain entry to the new church, the Kirk Session ensured that no work was carried out on Sundays.

At the beginning of 1972, several changes took place. The position of Church Officer, which had been vacant for a lengthy period, was filled by a member of the Men's Association, Tom Young. Tom thus became first Beadle of the new church, and served in that capacity for many years. Bill Gilmour replaced Mr Elliot as Home Board Missionary. Bill served for a number of years, and he and his wife attended several Boys' Brigade camps.

The new church building was finally ready. Last Communion in the old church took place on 4 June, and the new building was dedicated on 8 June by Rev. Stanley Mair, Moderator of Glasgow Presbytery. Rev. Jackie Stewart preached, and the Bible passages were read by Rev. Cran and Mr W. Smith, Session Clerk. Celebration socials were held in September. Thereafter, it was business as usual. Youth and adult organisations made good progress. As result of the Parish Visit, several new Sunday Schoolteachers and Boys' Brigade officers were recruited. One was Bob Wilson who succeeded Jim Halley as Boys' Brigade captain. Over 300 children attended monthly film shows organised by the Ways and Means committee.

The local Girl Guides requested the use of the church for Thinking Day. The request was granted, and this has become an annual event. Things were going really well for Springfield Cambridge Church. Perhaps too well.

Chapter 18
The wind of change

Problems were being encountered and changes were to take place or were being considered, during the last quarter of 1972, both at the church and in Bishopbriggs. Considerations were being given to selling the manse, which was proving costly to maintain. There were problems with the acoustics in the new church. Also, there was a shortfall in funds available to pay for the new building, so a "Wipe it out" appeal was set up to clear the accrued debt. While the fabric was giving rise for concern, the spiritual side of church life progressed. The Youth Fellowship was replaced by a Youth Club, at the request of the young people. One of the church Office-Bearers, Bob Leadbitter, offered to lead this group. In addition, a Crusaders' Bible Class met on Sunday afternoons.

Changes were taking place in Bishopbriggs also. Moves were afoot to start a Community Council. This is a non-political organisation, the function of which is to make representation on issues concerning the community and to organise functions such as gala days, memorial services etc. The church has been well represented on this body throughout the years. About the same time, the first and only Minister of the Gospel was elected member of Bishopbriggs Burgh Council. He was Rev. Geoff Scobie of St James the Less.

In January 1973 the Communion Roll was revised and it was established that membership stood at 1357. By that time, twenty-five young people had joined the Youth Club. All seemed to be going well when, sad to say, Rev. Cran was seriously injured by a lorry when crossing Kirkintilloch Road at Bishopbriggs Cross. The congregation was shocked, but quickly lent spiritual support. The Cambridge Chapel was opened daily for prayer and meditation, and no fewer that 840 members and 21 visitors attended the February Communion. There was no doubt about the severity of Rev. Cran's injuries. One of the local doctors had been passing at the time and was convinced that there was little or no hope. Some five weeks later there was better news, the Minister was out of danger. Recovery, however, would be slow. By May, he was allowed home to recuperate.

Meanwhile, many things were happening at the church. Kirking of the Council took place on 6 May. Popular organist, James McKee, resigned. He was sadly missed, not only for his fine playing and leadership of the choir, but also for the other work that he did, such as organising Congregational Cruises. One of the-office bearers, Mervin Porter, was elected President of the Glasgow Men's Association. Mervin also set up a church library. A church "Fayer" was held that year and raised £625. Welcome guests at that event were Rev. and Mrs Cran. Although not ready to resume duties Rev. Cran attended the September meeting of the Kirk Session and was again made most welcome. Another welcome visitor to Bishopbriggs that year was Princess Anne. She opened the Sports Centre on 12 July. This was one of her first solo visits to Scotland.

The third edition of the Church Hymnal was published in 1973 but was not adopted by Springfield Cambridge until some time later. Not that the church was opposed to innovation and change. Consideration was given to mount bells or chimes on the new church. This, however, proved impractical. Attention was paid to enhancing the internal furnishings. A cross from Springfield Church was refurbished and mounted above the pulpit in the new church. A Baptismal Font was donated by the Youth Organisations. The Woman's Guild and Young Wives donated a Communion Table Scarf.

Sad to say, the Youth Club ceased to function towards the end of that year but was reconstituted later. On the other hand, numbers attending Sunday School had increased to such an extent that yet another appeal for teachers had to be made. Just before the end of the year, Hector Sime resigned from the 'Ways and Means' committee. He was replaced by Mrs Pickett, who has served in that capacity for many years. This committee not only organises fund-raising ventures but also contributes greatly to the social life of the congregation.

By the beginning of 1974 there were 100 members in the Junior Section of the Boys' Brigade. Long time Officer-in-Charge, David Struthers, was an outstanding leader of young people. Meanwhile, Sunday School and all the other youth and adult organisations continued to make good progress. On 3 February, a woman minister conducted the evening Communion Service for the first time. She was Rev. Elizabeth Sutherland of Balornock North Church (now Wallacewell). Happy to say, Rev. Cran had recovered sufficiently to return to duty by the end of that month. Sad to say, his recovery was only partial. Mr Gilmour continued as assistant and organised an Elders' Training course at Crieff. This took place the following year.

Meanwhile, the Men's Association organised a Sporting Panel Night. One of the guests was Brian McGinlay, at that time the youngest referee in British senior football. One of the church elders, Drew Fleming, has also refereed at the highest level. Still the organisations continued to grow in membership. For example, there were 60 in the Shipmates, now the Anchor Boys. With such continued growth, it was agreed to upgrade the Springfield Hall, formerly the old church building.

1975 was the 268 Boys' Brigades' 40th Anniversary. By this time there were 110 boys in the Company Section. The Company did well that year. They won the Glasgow Battalion Senior Cross Country, and one of the boys, Lesley Johnston, won the Intermediate individual title. The Volleyball team won the Glasgow championship for the second time, then went on to be British Champions on two occasions. On the down side of church life, upkeep of the manse was proving costly. It was suggested that Strathkelvin District Council might like to buy it, but they declined. Bishopbriggs had become part of Strathkelvin in 1974. The "Kirking of the Council" took place at Springfield Cambridge in 1975. Towards the end of that year a Sunday Youth Club was formed. Its members drew up a constitution and presented it to the Kirk

Session for approval, which was duly given. So the year ended on a positive note.

At the beginning of 1976 St James the Less Episcopal Church was granted use of Cambridge Chapel for worship purposes until their new church was completed. They gifted a cross to Springfield Cambridge in token of appreciation. It is situated above the Communion Table in the Cambridge Chapel. This sharing of premises was but one example of inter-church co-operation. The three Church of Scotland Session Clerks met twice yearly to consider matters of mutual interest. Rev. Cran courageously continued his ministry but indicated that he would like to take early retirement if accommodation could be found for him. Despite his problems he and Mr Gilmour visited the newly occupied houses east of Woodhill Road.

A rather sad event took place that year. Ronald Dalgarno died. Ronald had been one of the founder staff members of the 268 Boys' Brigade and had served as captain for more than a decade, influencing many of the young men of the church. One of them, Councillor Vaughn, said of him - "He spread the Gospel Message by the example of his own Christian commitment".

It was not a good year for the church from a "Fabric" point of view. Cracks appeared on one of the walls of the church, and required urgent attention. Rear doors were vandalised, and had to be replaced with metal ones. There was also a small fire in the Cambridge Chapel one Sunday morning, but it was quickly extinguished and evacuation of the building was not required. It was also the year when Mr Gilmour moved to another charge. He and Mrs Gilmour were greatly missed by the congregation. In October, Rev. Cran attended his last board meeting. He preached his farewell sermon in November, the final act of a long career.

Chapter 19
The new minister

Rev. Bill Ewart B.Sc. B.D. preached as Sole Nominee on 20 November 1977. It was not his first charge, nor his first profession (Bill had been employed in the steel industry prior to his call to the ministry). It was the first time for many years, however, that "such a young man" had occupied the charge. With Bill came wife Ellen, daughter Allison and baby son Christopher. On that first Sunday few could have realised what an impact the manse family were going to have on Springfield Cambridge during the next 26 years. They settled in quickly and soon became part of church and community. The church was thriving in those days with 40 young people in Bible Class alone. At the other end of the youth scale a creché was established. Such events as Songs of Praise evening services were continued, as were many social and fund-raising activities. A new venture was undertaken when 81 members attended the Edinburgh Military Tattoo. Clearly there was a growing spirit of fellowship, friendship and enthusiasm in the church. This was reflected in that offerings increased by 31 per cent.

All in all, 1978 was a good year for Springfield Cambridge. It was the year in which the Boys' Brigade broadened its horizons and embarked on a wide range of activities which brought success during the following decade. In addition to Bible Class, Friday night activities and football, the boys became interested in swimming, athletics etc. A highly successful pipe band was established under Pipe Major Jim Pettigrew. It took part in many events and won numerous competitions. In addition to boys, quite a number of Girls Brigade members were introduced to piping. Another event, Cross Country, produced a rather unique family double when Billy Minto won the Glasgow Battalion Intermediate Championship in 1978, and brother Euan won the Junior title in 1982.

In 1979, Tom Callander of Tron St Marys Church undertook Readership training under Rev. Ewart. This was the first of many future Readers and Ministers to be trained at Springfield Cambridge under Bill's guidance. Bill must be given great credit for the training aspect of his ministry. Many future preachers benefited from his instruction and guidance. They include local ministers such as Mark Johnston (Kirkintilloch St Marys), David White (Kirkintilloch St Columbas), Diane Stewart (Milton of Campsie) and John MacGregor (formerly Wallacewell). Interestingly, one of Bills' last trainees was a Reader, a Mrs Ellen Ewart (Bill's wife)

Some rather interesting events took place locally in 1980. St James the Less Episcopal Church opened for worship. The Community Council assumed responsibility for Armistice and Remembrance day services, and have done so ever since. Louis Palau, the American Evangelist, took time off from his crusade in the Kelvin Hall to visit Collins's Publishers at Bishopbriggs. He was presented with a Bible to mark the occasion. Back at Springfield Cambridge, a no smoking rule was introduced. This was clear. Not so clear, however, is the meaning of a Congregational Board minute which states that a committee was to be set up to determine the optimum number of committees.

It was agreed to permit guide dog training to take place on the premises. The dog, or puppy as it was then, was trained by Mrs MacPhee and her family. This continued for many years, and all but one of the puppies passed the test to become guide dogs. Training of a different type was undertaken by three members of the congregation. They trained to be Readers. One of them, Bet Gregson, as previously mentioned, became a minister. Another, Jim Lockhart, had to demit after many years, due to failing eyesight, but continues his "ministry" as an Assistant Chaplin at Stobhill Hospital. Sad to say, 1980 did not end too well for Springfield Cambridge. A ten foot section of the manse garden wall collapsed, and had to be rebuilt. Worse was to follow. Major problems were discovered relating to the church roof. In the end, costly repairs had to be carried out.

1983 was the centenary of the founding of the Boys' Brigade. It was also the year when Mr George Younger, Board Member and former Burgh Councillor, wrote a letter to the Kirk Session proposing that women be admitted to the Eldership. No action was taken at the time but a statement was made later indicating that all church members age 21 and over are eligible for membership of the Kirk Session. Springfield Cambridge continued to prosper under Rev. Ewart, still referred to by many as "the new minister". Bill attended Boys' Brigade camp that year, and in many of the years that followed.

A most alarming incident took place one Sunday afternoon in February 1985. Intruders set fire to material stored in the cellar. Fortunately, Rev. Ewart had occasion to visit the premises about that time. He raised the alarm, and the fire was brought under control by the Fire Brigade. Unfortunately, vandalism was rife in Bishopbriggs at that time. History was made a month later when new Elders were admitted. Four of them were women. They were Anne Picket, Jessie MacKenzie, Elizabeth Gregson and Ann Harvey. This event was followed by an outreach to the Parish. Brochures were delivered to houses, and a series of services were held in Auchinairn and Woodhill Primary Schools.

In 1986, long serving Church Officer, Jim Tonner, was appointed. It was also the year when a group of office bearers, members and young people of the church spent a week-end together at St Ninian's Lay training centre, Crieff. 1987 will long be remembered, however, as the year when morning service was broadcast live on B.B.C. radio. The service was well led by Rev. Ewart, supported by an augmented choir and an enthusiastic congregation. That was also the year when the Woman's Guild celebrated its centenary. This was marked by national and local events. The Woman's Guild was actually founded by a man, Professor Archibald Charteris, who also founded *Life and Work*. Since 1887 the Church has benefited greatly from the talents, work and prayers of the women in the Guild. The Guild has seen many changes in its long and distinguished history and became the Church of Scotland Guild, following a review of procedure in 1997. Springfield Cambridge Woman's Guild organised short holidays at Craigengower for older ladies of the congregation. 1988 was the year of the Glasgow Garden Festival, and Springfield Cambridge won First Prize (A Rosebowl) in the in-door-garden competition for churches.

As the decade grew to a close, one wondered what the future would bring to the church, the congregation and the no longer new minister.

Guild at Craigengower 1989.

Chapter 20
Looking back, looking forward

The 1990s saw many changes at Springfield Cambridge church. Sad to say, the Young Women's Group discontinued. This group was founded in 1963 when the minister, Rev. French, approached Betty MacPhee, asking her to start a Young Wives and Mothers' Group. First meeting took place in 1964 when 30 attended. It adopted a constitution recommended by the Woman's Guild. Membership rose to over 100 during the 1970s. It offered fellowship and a wide range of activities. Visiting speakers included a young minister by the name of Sandy MacDonald (later to be Moderator of the General assembly of the Church of Scotland), and Ian Jackson, a consultant plastic surgeon (Later Professor Jackson of Boy David fame).

Unfortunately, membership dwindled towards the end of the 1980s, and a decision was taken to wind up the organisation in 1990. It had served its purpose by providing fellowship for mothers when their families were young. Many of its members became Sunday School Teachers, Girls' Brigade Officers, members of Congregational Board and Kirk Session and, of course, members of the Guild.

* * *

Helen Hamilton became Assistant Minister in 1990. She approached Audrey Minto and a few others about starting a Wall Hanging Group. The idea was to make four Wall Hangings, each depicting a Gospel, a season and a church festival. About twenty ladies expressed interest, and the project began. Men were not entirely excluded. Andrew Strang provided drawings, George Stevens made frames, and Donald MacPhee gave a substantial donation towards providing material etc. The ladies met. Each Gospel was read and studied. The first wall hanging was based on Matthew's Gospel, incorporating Winter, the Nativity and Love. It became obvious that the intricate work required would not be completed by Christmas, so it was set aside, and the ladies concentrated on the Easter theme from John's Gospel, incorporating Spring, Creation, and the Resurrection. It was completed and dedicated by Spring, 1991.

Rev. Helen Hamilton was called to be minister at St James's Pollok, but the group continued under the leadership of Audrey Minto. Sad to say, Audrey died later that year, but the Wall Hanging was completed and dedicated to her memory at Christmas, 1991. Anne Harvey became group co-ordinator. Work began on the autumn theme, taken from Luke's Gospel and incorporating Communion and Harvest Thanksgiving. It was dedicated in September 1993. Work then began on the Summer Wall Hanging. It was based on Mark's Gospel, and included Pentecost and Baptism. The dove on this hanging was handmade by Margaret Dalgleish. It was completed by June

1994. With the remaining funds a new cover was obtained for the Communion Table and the medallions from the original table sewn onto it.

* * *

Returning to other matters, a church library was set up in the Hall of Fellowship in 1990. It was also agreed to purchase a new organ that year. Unfortunately, it was also the year in which the Church Architect reported that repairs costing in the region of £43,000 were required, £21,000 urgently. Springfield Cambridge faced up to its responsibilities, and also saw its way to contribute to other causes. In 1991 for example, £1400 was raised for UNICEF, the Youth Fellowship contributed £130 to the Rumanian appeal, the Bible Class held a "bake for Bibles" coffee morning, the Junior Brigade raised £345 for World Mission Fund (this would please the church's Missionary Partner, Helen Scott), and £600 was raised for the Crisis in Africa appeal (£300 by a Sunday School sponsored silence).

This pattern of giving continued despite great demands on church funds. Another feature of those years, as previously mentioned, was the number of trainee ministers assigned to the church. A rather unusual incident took place when Mark Johnston was Assistant. It had been agreed to hold a fire drill at the end of service one Sunday morning. The elder conducting the drill stood outside to monitor evacuation time. It seemed to be taking forever. On investigation it transpired that Minister and Assistant had positioned themselves at each of the fire exits in order to shake hands with the congregation as they usually did.

Rev. W. Ewart, Session and Board.

In 1993 the Centenary of the Girls' Brigade was celebrated and captain, Mrs Cuthbert, was congratulated on 38 years service as an officer. Mrs Pickett was elected President of the North District Council of the Woman's Guild, and a Parish Visitation took place.

* * *

In 1994, an Over Fifties group was constituted. It proved popular, and has continued well into the new Millennium. The group meets monthly. Meetings begin with a short act of devotion, generally followed by keep fit, then a talk, demonstration or other activity. There are also theme days such as Halloween, Burns Supper etc. All meetings ending with tea and an informal get together. There is an annual outing, and visits to places of interest. On one occasion the Group visited the Scottish Parliament and were entertained by the then M.S.P. Brian Fitzpatrick. There was also a walking section at one time, which explored the old railway line from Campsie Glen to Strathblane, walked round Mugdock Park, and walked the canal banks from Possil to Craigmarloch, in easy stages. Several members also gained Discovery Awards. This is the over-fifties equivalent of the Duke of Edinburgh Award.

* * *

Unfortunately, the Men's Association could not form a committee, and had to disband. So it was that half way through the decade, the church was meeting with mixed fortunes.

Chapter 21
Towards the millennium

By April 1995 the church kitchen had been upgraded to meet new Health and Safety regulations. A church fete took place in June. Parish visitations continued. A South African children's gospel choir performed in November. Bishopbriggs Churches together set up an ecumenical Bible study group in 1996. Several Springfield Cambridge members joined, and have remained members ever since. While the church continued to produce and deliver Christmas and Easter messages for several years, this was a task ultimately undertaken by Bishopbriggs Churches Together. They also assumed responsibility for producing and delivering a Millennium message and gift to every house in Bishopbriggs. The gift was a dove mounted on transparent, adhesive material. Many of them remain on windows and doors in the district to this day.

* * *

Falling numbers in Bible Class was giving rise for concern. Lynne Robertson sounded out some of the young people who were in P7–S4 at school, some of whom had fallen away from Sunday School and Bible Class. As a result, a meeting took place one Saturday evening at the home of Michael and Valerie Cooke. About 15 young people attended, enjoyed the hospitality, took part in Bible related games, decided that they would like to meet as a group, and called themselves the Bible Wayfinders. The first official meeting took place at the church, in Room One, the following morning. It was not long before the young people were playing a very active part in church life. They began by leading the Children's Address on the occasional Sunday Morning. They then went on to conduct an evening service and eventually to take a full morning service on special occasions. Out with Sunday, they visited a wide range of places of interest, and played an increasing part in church life.

* * *

Sad to say, Willie Smith, Session Clerk for more than forty years, died in 1996. He was succeeded by Willie McSheehy. Another prominent church member died in 1997. David Struthers had been Officer-in-Charge of the 268 Junior Section for many years. He was kindly, dedicated, and greatly respected throughout the Glasgow Battalion. David was gentle and soft spoken. No one quite knew how one word from him could silence 100 boys and attract their undivided attention.

As the century drew to a close, two tragic events took place, which were to influence procedures within the church. As a result of the Dunblane shootings, and other disturbing events, Bill Reynolds was appointed Child Protection Officer. The other tragic event was an outbreak of E-Coli food poisoning in Wishaw. This resulted in Mrs Ditty being appointed church Hygiene

Supervisor. On the brighter side, Frazer McCulloch and Ross MacDonald won the Glasgow Churches Gents' Doubles badminton title in 1999, and Frazer partnered Karen MacDonald to win the Mixed Doubles also.

So it was that the Millennium ended on a high note at Springfield Cambridge.

Chapter 22
2000 and beyond

Church and members marked the new Millennium in a variety of ways. For example, the Girls Brigade presented the church with an illuminated stained glass picture which was mounted in the Hall of Fellowship, above the entrance to the Cambridge Chapel. A concert was staged by the young people of the congregation, followed by another featuring members of all ages.

***

Music was to feature highly at the beginning of the Millennium. In Springfield Cambridge. New organist, Alan Craig, was appointed in August 2000. He re established weekly choir practise (which had fallen by the wayside). A special

The History of the Millennium Gift to Springfield Cambridge Church

A Girls' Brigade Officer had an idea to have a show to celebrate the Millennium. A suggestion was made to involve all the youth organisations in the Church.

Around 200 children from The Boys' Brigade, The Girls' Brigade and Sunday Schools became involved. After a lot of hard work during the rehearsals by the children and the youth leaders the show took place on 27th & 28th January 2000 in Springfield Cambridge Church.

The show consisted of songs, dances, sketches and Boys' Brigade band all performed by the children.

Later the children were asked to design or discuss their ideas for a picture to be made for the church as a celebration for the Millennium. It transpired that a lot of the children had similar ideas i.e.. birds, candles, sun, bibles, rainbows and the world. Various pictures and ideas were given to a local stain glass studio. Gary J. Millington, from Authentic Stain Glass designed the above picture using the drawings from the children.

This stain glass picture was gifted to the Church from
  " The Youth of The Church" on Sunday 10th June 2001.

musical contribution to morning service was also re-introduced. Organist and Choir collaborated with the existing Praise Group to enhance worship. During December 2001, the first Christmas Presentation in aid of children's charity, C.H.A.S., took place. Gifted professional musicians gave their services free of charge. The choir was augmented by singers from choirs throughout the district. All this resulted in a wonderful evenings entertainment, enjoyed by an audience that packed the church to overflowing. Similar ventures have taken place in the following years and over £14,500 raised in total.

The choir moved to the balcony in 2002. This greatly enhanced acoustics. In August 2004, Choir and Praise Group formulated an agreement to become known as the Church Praise Team. So to 2005 when, in the words of Alan Craig, "The Church Praise Team continues to plough new furrows in its attempt to fuse old and new, and to allow young and old to find relevance in the church".

* * *

All groups and organisations have continued to progress and prosper during the first five years of the new Millennium. Of the adult groups, the Guild, the Caring Group and the Over Fifties continue to meet on the church premises. There is no longer a Men's Association, but several Springfield Cambridge members have joined the Cadder Men's Association, and greatly enjoy the fellowship experienced there. The Badminton Club continues to meet with considerable success in both local and national competitions.

So far as the young people are concerned, Sunday Schools, Bible Wayfinders, Boys' Brigade and Girls' Brigade continue to meet. The Girls' Brigade has been highly successful in Battalion and District competitions during the last few years but, like all the other organisations, its most important function is its weekly Christian witness to the young people of Bishopbriggs. A Youth Fellowship was re established in 2004. Its president, Douglas Robertson, spoke at the General Assembly of the Church of Scotland in 2005.

* * *

2003 saw significant changes in the Church of Scotland. That was the year when Rev. Adah Younger became first woman Moderator of Glasgow Presbytery. Dr. Alison Elliot became first woman Moderator of the General Assembly of the Church of Scotland. She was also the first lay person to hold that post for over 400 years.

Back at Springfield Cambridge, Rev. and Mrs Ewart presented the church with a Memorial Book. It is kept in the Cambridge Chapel, and is maintained by Session Clerk, Malcolm Galston. In the following year, Rev. Ewart received a call from a charge in Perthshire. He answered the call and moved on after 26 years at Springfield Cambridge. So it was that the church became vacant once again. It is interesting to note, however, that on this occasion, Interim Moderator, Rev. Mark Johnstone, and Locum, Alex Stuart, both undertook part of their training at Springfield Cambridge.

As this history ends, the church looks back with pride and thanksgiving for the past, and also looks forward to the future with anticipation, and confidence.

Sources

Minutes of Springfield Church of Scotland Kirk Session and Deacons Court meetings. Archives and Special Collections Section, Mitchell Library, Glasgow.

Minutes of Springfield Cambridge Church of Scotland Kirk Session and Congregational Board meetings. Springfield Cambridge Church Archives.

Rt. Rev. A. Herron. *Historical Directory to Glasgow Presbytery*. (1984). Glasgow Presbytery Office.

Indexed Files of *Kirkintilloch Herald*. East Dunbartonshire Information and Archives, Kirkintilloch.

Files of *Bishopbriggs News*. East Dunbartonshire Information and Archives, Kirkintilloch.

Springfield Church of Scotland, 90th Anniversary Report. (1955).

Springfield Cambridge Brochure. (1972).

Donald Armour, *History of 268 B.B. 1935–1985*. (1985).

Index

Anchor Boys: 46, 53
Armstrong, John: 23
Armstrong, Miss Annie: 34
Auchinairn: 7–9, 11–14, 16–21, 23, 24, 26, 28, 30, 56
Auchinairn Hall: 18, 19, 24, 26, 29, 31, 32, 36, 37

Badminton Club: 19, 37, 64
Band of Hope: 13, 23, 27
Bearyards Farm: 7, 40
Bible Wayfinders: 61, 64
Bishopbriggs Church: 12
Bishopbriggs Free Church: 8, 11, 34
Boys' Brigade: 27, 32, 33, 36–40, 43, 45, 49–51, 53–56, 64

Cadder Church: 7, 15
Cadder Free Church: 8, 9, 11, 12
Cambridge Street Church: 46–50
Cameron, Rev. John: 30, 32, 36
Caring Group: 64
Chalmers, Mrs: 33
Choir: 13, 15, 16, 44, 50, 56, 63, 64
Church Praise Team: 64
Congregational Board: 26, 45, 49, 56, 58
Cran, Rev. James: 47–49, 51–54

Davie, John: 27, 33
Deacons' Court: 18, 24, 39, 42, 43
Disruption: 7

Ewart, Rev. Bill: 55, 56, *59*, 64

Fordyce, Rev. James: 8, 9
Free Church: 7, 10, 13, 15
French, Rev. Henry J.: 37–40, 42–44, 58

Girls' Association: 23, 24, 26, 29, 30, 32, 33
Girls' Guildry: 38, 39
Guild: 23, 26, 32, 64

Hebenton, Rev. David: 44–46

Jellyhill: 11, 26, 30

Kelly, Rev. J. Watson: 19
Kenmure Church: 18
Kenmure Men's Own: 24, 38, 39
Kenmure United Free Church: 13, 15
"Kist-o-Whistles": 24, 46

Life Boys: 27, 29, 43
Lindsay, Rev. William: 11, 12, 16, 17
Lochfaulds: 11, 26

MacKinnon, John: 36
Martin, Rev. Donald: 23, 24, 26, 27, 29, 30, 32
Mavis Valley: 11, 12, 14, 16, 26, 30
Men's Association: 46, 49, 50, 52, 53, 60

Neilson, Rev. Thomas: 16, 18

Over Fifties: 60, 64

Primrose, Rev. Robert: 20, 21

Reid, Rev. R. W.: 12–14
Relief Church: 7

Secession: 7
Shipmates: 46, 53
"Sleeping Hollow": 11, 12

Smith, William: 27, 39, 51, 61
Sounding board: 33, 37
Springfield Cambridge Church: 33, 48–51, 53, 55, 56, 58, 59, 63, 64
St James the Less: 52, 54, 55
Stirling, James K.: 19, 30
Sutherland, Rev. Lewis A.: 18, 19, 32, 38, 39

Taylor, Rev. Henry: 15

United Presbyterian Church: 13, 15, 47

Wall Hanging(s): 58
Watt, Rev.: 15
Woman's Guild: 26, 53, 56, 58, 60

Young Wives: 43, 53, 58
Young Worshippers' League: 40, 49
Younger, George: 26, 56
Youth Club: 52, 53
Youth Fellowship: 41, 42, 52, 59, 64